Yearbook
2008

✚ 2007 CONTENTS

118

27

34

76

107

4 HEADLINES From Virginia Tech and the disappearance of Madeleine McCann to the $12 million dog and the wild-girl antics of Britney, Lindsay and Paris: more than 40 memorable stories from 2007

50 WEDDINGS Liz Hurley had two: one in England and one in India (with dancing horses and millions of chili peppers). Eva Longoria and Tony Parker celebrate in a 17th-century French château; Rebecca Romijn and Jerry O'Connell choose hay bales and provide flip-flops

62 ROMANCES *High School Musical*'s Zac Efron and Vanessa Hudgens splash around like teenagers in love; Chris Evert and Greg Norman go public; *Melrose Place* lovers Heather Locklear and Jack Wagner date for real; and more

68 BABIES As Patrick Dempsey, Marcia Cross, Diddy and Elvis Costello know well, 2007 was the Year of Twins

84 SPLITS Michelle Williams and Heath Ledger make the biggest headlines; Denise Richards and Richie Sambora

20

138

may have been the most amicable; and Anne Heche and Coley Laffoon lob legal grenades

90 TELEVISION The year belonged to *High School Musical, Hannah Montana* and . . . Sanjaya?

96 MOVIES Abdominal showmen make *300* a hit, and *Pirates, Shrek* and *Bourne* scored big with sequel sequels

98 MUSIC Carrie Underwood proves she is anything but an underdog; an *Idol* also-ran comes out on top; the Police

return to duty after a long furlough; 50 Cent and Kanye duke it out

102 STYLE Glam gowns from Oscar, Emmy and Golden Globe red carpets, as worn by Reese, Eva, Angelina, Nicole and Beyoncé. Plus: Some not-so-haute couture

118 FAREWELL Remembering the eventful lives of James Brown, Gerald Ford, Merv Griffin, Luciano Pavarotti, Deborah Kerr, Norman Mailer, Robert Goulet, Alex the parrot and many more

95

■ **VIRGINIA TECH MASSACRE**
April 16

Headlines
2007

'/////////////.

The day after one of the worst mass murders in U.S. history, thousands of students gathered to mourn the dead.

Tragedy Beyond Words

A gunman's senseless rampage at Virginia Tech left 32 students and teachers dead, a campus wounded and one agonizing, perhaps unanswerable question: Why?

Disturbing images of Cho surfaced after the killings; mourners (below) grieved at a makeshift memorial.

"We heard the shots getting closer, moving toward us, down the hallway," said Andrey Andreyev, 19, an engineering student at Virginia Tech. "Once we heard the screams, there were no longer any questions about what was happening."

What was happening was horror beyond comprehension: Seung-Hui Cho, a 23-year-old student with a history of psychological problems, was walking the floors of the engineering building, shooting students and teachers at random and without mercy. "He took his time in between each shot," said a survivor. "After each shot I'd hear a quick moan, or a grunt, or a quiet yell." Before it was over, 32 had died, including Professor Liviu Librescu, 76, a Holocaust survivor who had barred the classroom door with his body while some of his students escaped through the windows.

Cho shot himself as police finally entered the building. While an investigation of his psychological history showed depression and suicidal thoughts, nothing predicted the cataclysm that was to come.

Student Kevin Sterne, severely wounded, was rushed to a hospital. He lived.

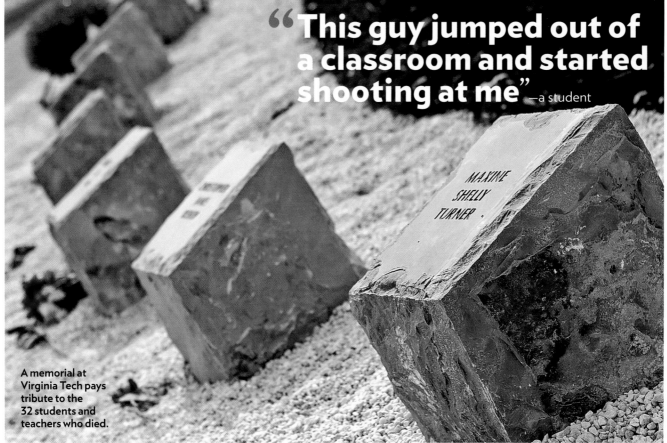

"This guy jumped out of a classroom and started shooting at me" —a student

A memorial at Virginia Tech pays tribute to the 32 students and teachers who died.

MAXINE
SHELLY
TURNER

Smith parlayed a studied
pout and cartoon figure into
a kind of tabloid stardom.

Farewell, Anna Nicole

In a lifetime quest for fame, the surgically enhanced, geezer-marrying stripper turned *Playboy* model left almost no cliché unlived

"She was searching for a family, something she never had" —a friend

Scenes from a sad circus: Stern, Dannielynn and Anna Nicole in 2006; Birkhead celebrating his paternity-hearing victory.

Clockwise from top: the casket; Anna Nicole's final resting place in the Bahamas; and mom Virgie Arthur at the funeral.

Ready? And *inhale* . . .

On Feb. 8, 154 days after the birth of her daughter Dannielynn and 151 days after the death of her son Daniel, 20, from a drug overdose, actress-model-personality Anna Nicole Smith, 39, collapsed and died in Florida. Her lover Howard K. Stern; her mother, Virgie Arthur; and a former lover, Larry Birkhead, who claimed to be Dannielynn's real father, fought over custody of the child (who may or may not someday inherit a chunk of the $1.6 billion estate of Smith's late husband, Texas oil baron J. Howard Marshall II) and where Smith would be buried. Twenty-two days later, after contentious legal squabbling, Smith—in a casket covered in a tassled pink cloth decorated with a smiley face made from Swarovski crystals—was finally buried in the Bahamas. (Virgie Arthur tried to stop the funeral at the last moment and was later booed outside the church.) On March 26 the Florida medical examiner ruled that Smith had died from an accidental overdose of nine drugs; on April 10 a Bahamian court ruled that DNA tests had proved Birkhead was Dannielynn's father. Birkhead and Stern worked out an agreement wherein Stern will be the executor of Anna Nicole's estate. Dannielynn, who turned 1 on Sept. 7, is now living with Birkhead.
And *exhale* . . .

■ *May 3*

McCann Mystery

We're just praying and praying," said the little girl's grandmother, early in the case, "and hoping that we'll get Madeleine back."

Months later, the disappearance of Madeleine McCann, 3—who apparently vanished from her bed in a Portuguese resort while her parents, British physicians Kate and Gerry McCann, both 38, dined with friends a few hundred feet away—is still a mystery. Thanks in part to the couple's persistence, the case made worldwide headlines, and celebs from J.K. Rowling to Simon Cowell volunteered to help. But despite an intense international effort, authorities seem to have found little of substance, and each month brings a tantalizing—or shocking—new theory. (A tourist snap of a little girl in Morocco who looked like Maddy turned out to be the daughter of an olive grower; in September, Portuguese officials announced that the McCanns themselves were suspects, but the evidence—DNA found in a rented car—now seems less conclusive.)

At the McCanns' home in Leicestershire, the child's room remains untouched. Says a relative: "They want to keep things in place for Madeleine when she comes home."

Kate and Gerrry McCann are "both coping, keeping each other afloat," said a friend.

"**Please, please, do not hurt her. . . . Please give our little girl back**"
—Kate McCann

"The answers that everybody wants, we may never have"

—D.A. Scott Ballard

June 24

A Wrestler's Rage

Chris and Daniel Benoit at a ceremony honoring the wrestler in 2004. "Daniel worshipped his dad," said a former neighbor. Below: Nancy Benoit.

I n a weekend rampage starting on June 22, World Wrestling Entertainment champion Chris Benoit, 40, killed his wife, Nancy, 43, his son Daniel, 7, and himself in their suburban Atlanta home. Months later no one knows why.

There had been trouble in the past: Nancy had filed for divorce in 2003, claiming Chris had threatened her, but the couple reconciled; she had also been charged, in an earlier marriage, with attacking her then-husband with a knife. A spokesman for the WWE claimed Daniel had an autism-related medical condition, fragile X syndrome, and that the couple had been arguing about his proper care; Nancy's parents said Daniel was a "normal child with no health problems," and his medical records showed no evidence of serious illness. An investigation into the possibility of "'roid rage" proved inconclusive: An autopsy showed no trace of anabolic steroids, but Chris's body did have 10 times the normal level of testosterone, as well as therapeutic amounts of Xanax and the painkiller hydrocodone. "There are thousands of men walking around now with the same levels of testosterone," said Georgia's Chief Medical Examiner Kris Sperry, who noted such dosages are commonly prescribed to replenish low testosterone levels. "There is no way to know if the combination of the drugs affected his behavior."

The only sad, awful comfort? Daniel's blood also contained Xanax. "To think Daniel might not have known or been conscious when he died," said Richard Decker, an attorney representing Nancy's family, "is, in a strange way, a relief."

Edwards's message? "Don't stop living," she says. "Live until you die."

Hope and Courage

The strongest person in the presidential primaries? It may well be Elizabeth Edwards, Democratic hopeful John Edwards's wife. Three years ago Elizabeth was diagnosed with, and survived, breast cancer. Last March the cancer returned, and it's incurable. She doesn't know how long she has, but, focusing on her husband and three children (Cate, 25, Emma Claire, 9, and Jack, 7), Elizabeth lives her life with grace, energy and even humor. "I tell [my] doctors all the time, 'My job is to stay alive until you find an answer,'" she said. "'And your job is to find an answer quickly.'"

■ *January 2*

HERO AT THE STATION

Waiting on a Harlem platform, Wesley Autrey saw film student Cameron Hollopeter suffer a seizure and fall onto the tracks. "The downtown train was coming," recalled the genial Navy vet. "I'm thinking, 'Somebody's got to help this guy.' My mind said, 'Fool, you the only one here.'" Autrey leaped onto the tracks and, with the train less than 10 feet away, pinned down the thrashing Hollopeter in a 21-in.-deep drainage trough between the rails. "The first car rubbed the cap I was wearing. I'm like, 'Sir, I don't know you and you don't know me, but please don't move.'" To Autrey's eternal relief, "I'm 175 lbs. If I'd been carrying more weight…"

Autrey's heroics won him instant celebrity, with appearances on *Letterman* and *Ellen*, a $10,000 check from Donald Trump and a U.S. Senate resolution in his honor. "What better way to start out the new year," he said, "than to save somebody's life?"

"My mom raised me where if you see someone hurt or in need, you don't walk away," said Autrey.

■ *January*

Keith & Nicole

Now there's a year: In June 2006 Keith
Urban married Nicole Kidman. Just four
months later, startling almost everyone,
he fell off the wagon and checked
himself into the Betty Ford Center, where he stayed
for 90 long days. What happened? "I was going to
lose it all," he told PEOPLE months later. "It was like,
'If I don't choose this moment to do the right thing
and do something that's going to give me life, all
of the things I'm scared of losing, I'm going to lose
anyway.'" Urban and Kidman, both 40, have said
that his struggle, in the end, made their marriage
stronger. "Oh God yeah," says Urban. "It's like
moving into a house and the house burns down: We
get to build a new one together. . . . We know every
part of [our relationship] because we've built it. Just
the two of us. It's beautiful." He was overwhelmed,
and grateful, that Kidman stood by him: "Nicole
listened to her heart and did what she felt was the
right thing to do. To see that kind of love in action
. . . just makes me want to be a better man."

■ *August*
30 LBS. LIGHTER

Valerie Bertinelli

F ollowing in the (75 lbs. lighter) footsteps of Kirstie Alley, Valerie Bertinelli became the latest celeb to publicly promise to lose significant weight as the face of the Jenny Craig diet line. In five months she dropped 30 lbs. Her new goal? A total of 40 lbs. down. Her look-good-on-the-red-carpet trick? "I wear Spanx [slimming lingerie]," she said. "Here's a milestone: I'm now wearing small Spanx, not large!"

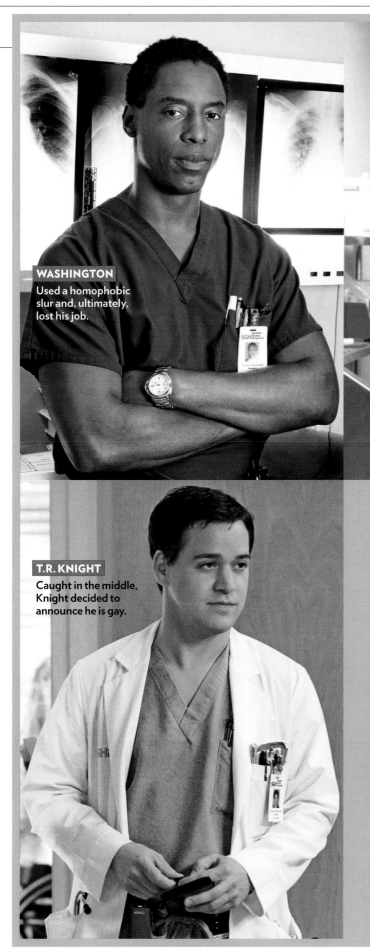

Anatomy
of an *Anatomy*
Scandal

June

In October 2006, during an argument with co-star Patrick Dempsey, *Grey's Anatomy*'s Isaiah Washington used a homophobic slur to describe castmate T.R. Knight. Publicly, Washington at first sought to downplay the incident; when talk of the scandal grew, he issued a public apology ("I sincerely regret my actions"), met with gay-rights groups, made a public service announcement and entered a counseling program.

Alas, the treatment didn't save the patient: In June Washington, 44, was stunned to learn that his contract would not be renewed. As his agent told tvguide.com, "[If] you did everything that was asked of you, and then they still kick you in the gut? How would you feel?" (NBC later signed Washington for five episodes of *Bionic Woman*. "He has learned his lesson," said an NBC exec. "He deserves a second chance.")

"It definitely crossed my mind we might die"

—survivor Adam Taki

Tress Goodwin (far left) sits in the ashes of her parents' house near San Diego. The blazes burned more than 465,000 acres and caused at least $1.5 billion in damage.

California wildfires

When fall comes to Southern California, hot Santa Ana winds can fan a spark into an inferno. But even longtime residents were stunned by this year's version, when gusts up to 100 mph hurled fireballs down the canyons. Nearly a million people were evacuated and more than 2,000 homes destroyed. "It was midnight, and the fire came out of nowhere," said Adam Taki, 23, whose experience in Malibu was shared by thousands. "It struck like lightning. It wasn't a brush fire; it was a firestorm—a tornado of fire that swooped through the whole neighborhood.... There were 60- to 75-ft. flames flying over the house. All our palm trees were on fire." Running wasn't an option. "There was nowhere we could go," said Taki. "We were at the windows letting the firemen know we were there. They shouted, 'Stay in the house! Do not move!' It was the scariest 45 minutes of my life. It definitely crossed my mind we might die there. Especially when, after the storm, the firemen said they'd been scared. They said at one point it was so hot they were about to jump in the house and stand there with us."

DAVID EVANS

READE SELIGMANN

COLLIN FINNERTY

■ *June*

Duke
Debacle

A nd the 2007 Spectacular Implosion Award goes to: Durham County, N.C., District Attorney Mike Nifong, 57, who launched the incendiary Duke rape case in 2006. A year later Nifong—who had been running for office when he filed charges—was found by a disciplinary committee to have withheld DNA evidence that might have exonerated the three accused lacrosse players. On June 16 he was disbarred; on July 2 he resigned; on Oct. 5 the players—Reade Seligmann, Collin Finnerty and David Evans—sued Nifong and others for unspecified damages. "We can draw no other conclusion," said the chairman of the ethics panel, than that "those initial statements he made were to further his political ambitions."

MIKE NIFONG

"Fiasco"
— the chairman of the disciplinary panel's assessment of the case

Familiar accessories: a handcuffed Simpson was taken to jail in Las Vegas on Sept. 16.

Back to Court

O.J. Simpson was back in handcuffs following a bizarre incident in a Las Vegas hotel-casino. Simpson said he went to the Palace Station to confront memorabilia dealers Alfred Beardsley and Bruce Fromong, whom Simpson, 60, claimed were selling items stolen from him. Beardsley told police that several men, accompanied by Simpson, burst into his room and threatened him at gunpoint. Six men were arrested; three have since pleaded guilty to reduced charges and agreed to testify against Simpson, who could face life in prison when he and his cohorts are tried in 2008.

■ September 19

WINKLER: 155 DAYS

On March 22, 2006, Mary Winkler killed her husband, Rev. Matthew Winkler, with a shotgun. On April 19, 2007, she was convicted of voluntary manslaughter—not murder—and, later, given a three-year sentence. The Selmer, Tenn., jury apparently believed Winkler's testimony that she killed her husband during a blackout after years of emotional and physical abuse. Not everyone was happy with the verdict. "None of us will ever know what the whole truth was," said a member of Matthew's church. "Matthew never got a chance to stand up and speak for himself."

Winkler was released from jail after serving 155 days (she will be on probation for 2 ½ years). In September she was granted the right to have supervised visits with her daughters, Patricia, 10 (who testified for the prosecution), Allie, 8, and Brianna, 2.

"We should be together," Winkler said of her children, whose father she killed, "because we need to talk this out."

Spears checked into rehab on Feb. 20 but walked out less than 24 hours later. That night, trailed by about 20 paparazzi, she showed up outside the home of her ex-husband Kevin Federline at about 7 p.m. He didn't appear, so Spears left. But when a photographer followed her to a gas station, Spears became enraged and began whacking his SUV with an umbrella. She returned to rehab that night. "Britney scared everyone real bad," said a Federline friend.

Girls gone wild!

It seems like only yesterday they were young, fresh-faced, innocent. And then . . . stuff happened

September 9

Spears tottered through a dance routine at the VMAs. A witness said she showed up late for rehearsals, carrying two empty margarita glasses.

February 16

Spears walked into a random Tarzana, Calif., salon, borrowed clippers and shaved her head—stunning family, friends and fans. She had "no expression, like flatlining," said the salon owner. "She is obviously in a lot of pain," said a friend, "and needs help immediately."

AUGUST 1999
The teen idol America loved.

Britney

September 30

With Preston, 2, and Jayden, 1, in their safety seats, Spears looked like a doting mom. But her erratic behavior temporarily cost her custody of the kids.

Paris

"I was basically in the fetal position, basically in hysterics," said Paris (in her mug shot, right) of trying to sleep in jail. She called her 23-day confinement "a really humbling experience."

ca. **1992**
Then, she lived a simpler life.

May 4

After a 2006 DUI arrest, Paris was caught driving with a suspended license (twice) and speeding, with her lights off. She was stunned when a judge sentenced her to 45 days in jail. "You're pathetic!" her mother shouted at prosecutors; comforting Paris, she added, "After we spent so much money!"

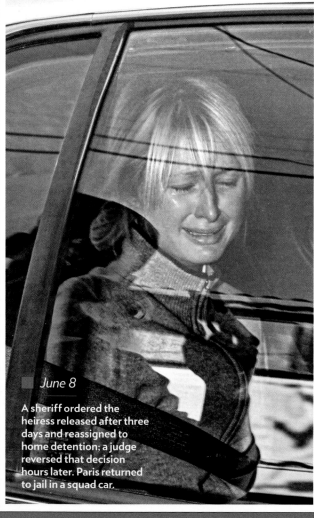

■ *June 8*

A sheriff ordered the heiress released after three days and reassigned to home detention; a judge reversed that decision hours later. Paris returned to jail in a squad car.

■ *June 26*

Leaving jail, said Paris, was like "a wedding day, like having a baby, that kind of happiness." Now, she added, "I'm grateful for everything. Even having a pillow."

May 26

A car crash led to DUI and drug charges and a second, 46-day stint in what her rep calls "an intensive medical rehabilitation facility." Earlier there had been photos of the actress allegedly using cocaine in a nightclub.

1998
The freckle-faced Disney girl.

Lindsay

 July 24

Lohan was arrested again (mug shot, above) for DUI and cocaine possession. She returned to rehab for the third time. "My life has become completely unmanageable," she said later, "because I am addicted to alcohol and drugs."

May 28

Soon after her crash, Lohan attended a private Hollywood party where, sources said, drugs were used. Paparazzi snapped a limp Lohan being driven home.

Summer 2006

At first, Lohan treated rehab as a "joke," said a friend. "After that, a lot of her friends [were] like, 'If she doesn't care, why should we?'"

■ *August 22*

Baby drama

Eight months after calling it quits, actress Bridget Moynahan and Super Bowl quarterback Tom Brady welcomed their baby John Edward Thomas Moynahan into the world. Awkward? Could be. The pair ended their three-year relationship last December, and Brady, 30, began dating supermodel Gisele Bündchen, 27. Only then did Moynahan, 36, discover she was pregnant. Both sides appear to be making the best of the situation. It was clear, says Brady friend Jason Taylor, that "these are adults who are responsible enough to work things out. Things happen, but they're handling it correctly."

■ *December 6, 2006*

A FATHER'S COURAGE

From a helicopter over the peaks of the Oregon Coast Range, rescuers suddenly saw what they had been praying for: Kati Kim, 30, waving an open umbrella to attract attention. Kim, her husband, James, 35, and daughters Penelope, 4, and Sabine, 7 months, had been missing in the wilderness for nine days after their car got stuck in the snow. Authorities had finally zeroed in by tracking James's cell-phone signal. "The fact that they were found is miraculous," said an elated official. "She was that smart to save her babies and herself."

Sadly, joy was tempered by tragedy. Two days earlier, desperate to save his family, James, an editor at the Web site CNET, had set out to find help. Searches found him on Dec. 6. Weak from lack of food—he made sure what little they had went to the children—he had died of exposure.

Kim (with Penelope, right, and Sabine) was "an insanely dedicated father," said a friend.

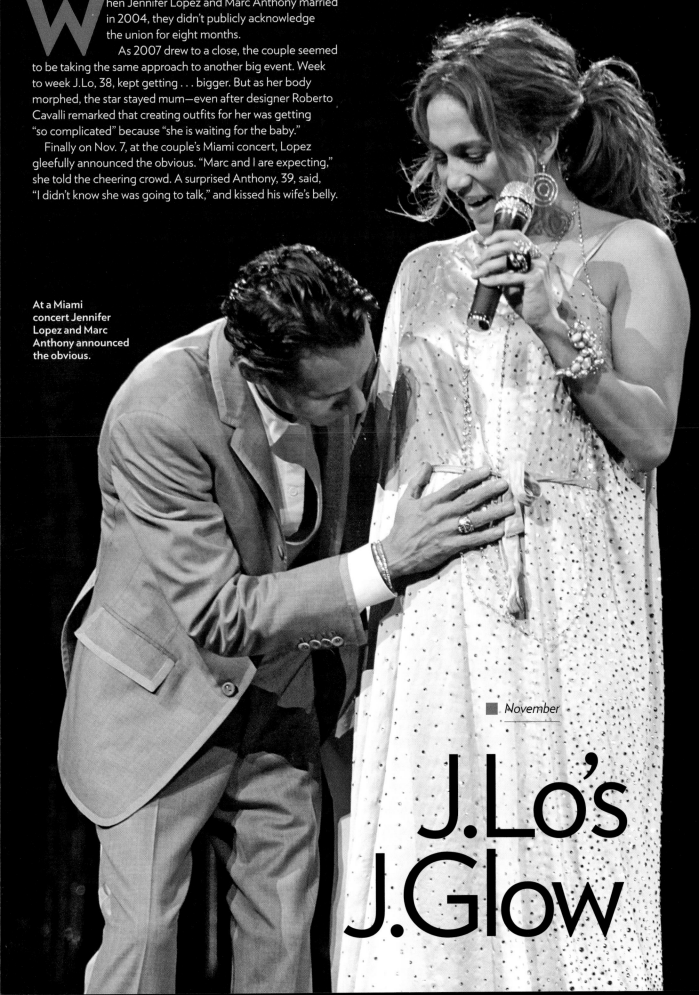

W hen Jennifer Lopez and Marc Anthony married in 2004, they didn't publicly acknowledge the union for eight months.

As 2007 drew to a close, the couple seemed to be taking the same approach to another big event. Week to week J.Lo, 38, kept getting . . . bigger. But as her body morphed, the star stayed mum—even after designer Roberto Cavalli remarked that creating outfits for her was getting "so complicated" because "she is waiting for the baby."

Finally on Nov. 7, at the couple's Miami concert, Lopez gleefully announced the obvious. "Marc and I are expecting," she told the cheering crowd. A surprised Anthony, 39, said, "I didn't know she was going to talk," and kissed his wife's belly.

At a Miami concert Jennifer Lopez and Marc Anthony announced the obvious.

■ November

J.Lo's J.Glow

Guzman and Partee somehow plunged from a *Grand Princess* balcony.

■ March 25

Emotional Rescue

ERNESTO GUZMAN

He said it as if the worst thing that happened were running out of margarita mix. "The cruise was great," a grinning Ernesto Guzman told PEOPLE moments after walking off the *Grand Princess.* "It was awesome."

No question about that—if by awesome you mean terrifying, death-defying and more than a little mystifying. For it was Guzman, 22, a U.S. Air Force Academy cadet, along with fellow passenger Clarice Partee, 20, a student at the University of Colorado, who on the festive first night of a spring break cruise somehow tumbled over a balcony railing and plunged 50 feet into the Gulf of Mexico, triggering a four-hour rescue that left passengers in tears.

"You could hear this distant, desperate cry"

—a passenger

Found Alive

On Jan. 8 William "Ben" Ownby was kidnapped in broad daylight in front of his family's Beaufort, Mo., home. Four days later FBI agents, acting on a tip, entered an apartment in a St. Louis suburb and found not only Ben but Shawn Hornbeck, 15, who had disappeared without a trace four years before while riding his bike. Michael Devlin, 41, a pizza-parlor manager whom friends described as a low-key loner, was arrested and, on Oct. 8, pleaded guilty to a long list of charges including kidnapping, forcible sodomy and attempted murder and received multiple life sentences.

(Devlin also confessed that he had kept Hornbeck, who had never contacted his parents even though he was only 50 miles away, under his control by threatening to kill him.) Both boys were reunited with their parents and are, reportedly, doing well.

DEVLIN

Guzman's buddies alerted officials, and Captain Ed Perrin turned the 109,000-ton boat around in 10 minutes. Hundreds of passengers scanned the night sea, but, said one, "it was like looking for two needles in a haystack."

Then at about 5 a.m. . . . a glimpse of someone in the water. Captain Perrin turned off the engines; suddenly "you could hear this distant, desperate cry," said passenger Jean Davis. "'Help me! Help me!'"

It was Partee, who was quickly rescued. Half an hour later, passengers heard Guzman. When he was brought safely aboard, said a passenger, "everyone erupted into cheers."

The pair were "just extremely lucky," said a Coast Guard spokesman. "No flotation devices, and then to be found in pitch dark—man, it's a miracle."

Shawn was reunited with his mom, Pam Akers; Devlin (above) pleaded guilty.

"We fought together, like we've done our whole lives," said Nell (with Jim near the site of the attack).

Teresa Earnhardt (right) said she was "disappointed that Dale Jr. has chosen to leave the family business."

Dale Earnhardt

When Dale Earnhardt Jr., NASCAR's most popular driver, announced that he was leaving the team founded by his late, legendary dad—and now run by his stepmom Teresa—he tried to take the high road. "She's a smart businesswoman and always tried to be fair," he said. Still, he admitted, "[Our relationship] has never been that great."

Junior, 33, insisted his decision to become a free agent stemmed from a desire to work for a company with the technology necessary to make him a more consistent winner. Others noted that there have been problems ever since Teresa wed Dale Sr., when Junior was a child. "They never got along," said Gary Hargett, one of Dale Sr.'s close friends.

"[My father] would understand my wanting to be where I could win," said Dale Jr., who on June 13 signed with Hendrick Motorsports.

■ *January 24*

Mountain Lion Attack!

Jim and Nell Hamm were hiking in Northern California, when all of a sudden he "heard a crunching sound." A moment later he was knocked to the ground by a 70-lb. mountain lion, which sunk its teeth into his head. As Jim stuck his hand into the cat's mouth to try to limit the damage, Nell, 65, grabbed a log and started clubbing the animal. "I really was afraid he was going to die," Nell said. "That what we were doing wasn't going to be enough."

When Jim, 70, yelled that he had a ballpoint pen in his pocket, she pulled it out and jabbed the lion in the eye; seeing that had no effect, she resumed hitting it with the log. To the couple's relief, the lion released Jim—but turned toward Nell. She raised her hands over her head—making herself appear larger—and yelled. The lion turned tail and vanished into the forest (and was later shot by state game officials).

Jim required a three-week hospital stay and four surgeries, but the pair are back to hiking in the area—though they now carry pocket knives. "When you come so close to losing everything, you become very thankful," Nell said. "That's what I feel today: thankful that Jim is here."

Craig's dilemma and explanations made Republican leaders furious and stand-up comics grateful.

■ *June 11*

LARRY CRAIG

Idaho's Larry Craig built a solid conservative reputation during 26 years on Capitol Hill, first in the House and, since 1991, in the Senate. It came crashing down after Craig, 62, married with three grown children, was arrested as part of a sex sting in a Minnesota airport men's room and pleaded guilty to disorderly conduct.

Under pressure from image-conscious Republicans, Craig, who insisted he was innocent but "panicked" and pleaded guilty to make the problem "go away," said he would resign quickly. Then he said he'd step down *if* he couldn't withdraw his plea. When a judge rejected his request, Craig, infuriating Republican leaders, reneged on his promise and said he planned to serve until his term ended in 2009.

In their NBC interview, when Harry commented on the complexity of their lives, William teased, "*You* may be abnormal. I'm pretty normal."

The Royals

For Princes William and Harry, 2007 brought romantic upheaval, a concert honoring their mom and their first American TV interview (a revelation: One of Harry's nicknames is 'Ginger')

June 18

The princes (with interviewer Matt Lauer) came off as smart, funny and droll.

March 16 ■

William and stylish, low-key Kate Middleton (at a horse race on March 16) split in the spring but were back together within weeks.

Prince William

////////////////////////////.

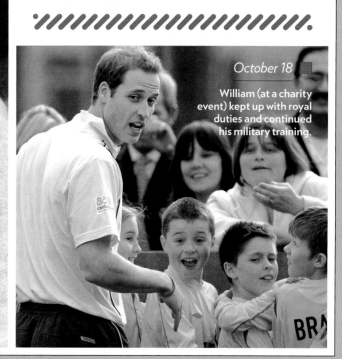

October 18 ■

William (at a charity event) kept up with royal duties and continued his military training.

July 1

To mark the 10th anniversary of Diana's death, Harry (with Kanye West) and William staged a concert to celebrate her life.

April 27

Harry and girlfriend Chelsy Davy (clubbing in London) reportedly split in November after three years.

"Oh, he's a wild thing all right. Yeah" —Prince William

June 10

During a break from military training in Canada, Harry fraternized with locals.

November 1

Citing the risk to fellow soldiers, officials decided not to send Harry (above, dive training) to Iraq.

August 31 ■

Harry greeted guests at
a service to commemorate
the life of his mother.

Prince
Harry

After his fourth DUI offense, the *24* star agreed to spend 48 days in jail.

■ *September*

Kiefer Sutherland

Pulled over for making an illegal U-turn in Hollywood on Sept. 25, Kiefer Sutherland was given a sobriety test, which he failed. The *24* star—already on probation for a 2004 DUI arrest, his third—pleaded no contest. Prosecutors recommended that he serve 18 days in jail for violating his probation and, before next July, another 30 days for his most recent offense. "I'm very disappointed in myself for the poor judgment I exhibited recently," the 41-year-old actor said in a statement, "and I'm deeply sorry for the disappointment and distress this has caused my family, friends and coworkers on *24* and at 20th Century Fox," the show's studio.

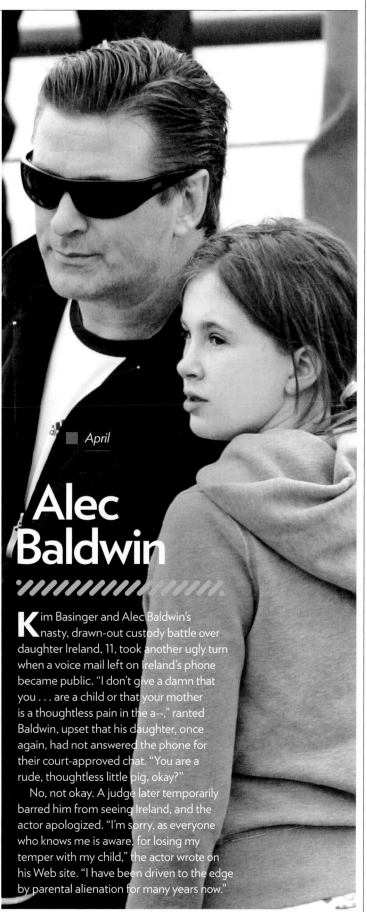

■ *May*

DAVID HASSELHOFF

Actor and rehab veteran David Hasselhoff, 55, admitted to falling off the wagon following the release of a video showing the apparently inebriated star lying on the floor struggling to eat a burger. "There was a tape made that night to show me what I was like [when drunk]," Hasselhoff said in a statement. "I have learned from it." An L.A. judge temporarily suspended visitation with his two daughters, Hayley, 15, and Taylor-Ann, 17, pending further review of the footage, on which his oldest is heard begging her dad to clean up his act. Hasselhoff regained visitation rights after agreeing to alcohol testing three times per week.

The disturbing tape of Hasselhoff became a Web sensation and forced him to make changes.

■ *April*

Alec Baldwin
//////////////////.

Kim Basinger and Alec Baldwin's nasty, drawn-out custody battle over daughter Ireland, 11, took another ugly turn when a voice mail left on Ireland's phone became public. "I don't give a damn that you . . . are a child or that your mother is a thoughtless pain in the a--," ranted Baldwin, upset that his daughter, once again, had not answered the phone for their court-approved chat. "You are a rude, thoughtless little pig, okay?"

No, not okay. A judge later temporarily barred him from seeing Ireland, and the actor apologized. "I'm sorry, as everyone who knows me is aware, for losing my temper with my child," the actor wrote on his Web site. "I have been driven to the edge by parental alienation for many years now."

The final straw for Rosie was a shouting match with Hasselbeck.

Exit
Rosie

■ *May 23*

That morning on *The View*, what began as typical sniping between Rosie O'Donnell and Elisabeth Hasselbeck quickly escalated into something else. "It was like watching a domestic dispute unfolding," said a witness. "It was really uncomfortable."

On the air O'Donnell, 45, accused her conservative cohost of not defending her against media criticism (O'Donnell's antiwar sentiments had drawn flack from right-wing pundits). The 10-minute fight ended in a split-screen shoutfest and turned out to be the last straw in O'Donnell's tumultuous eight-month *View* stint. Two days later ABC announced that O'Donnell had asked to be released from her contract; the network agreed to let her leave the show three weeks before her planned June 21 exit. "She was tired of the day-to-day fighting," said a friend.

Afterward Hasselbeck, 30, said she and Rosie were "friends." Not so, Rosie said on her blog: "I never tried harder . . . but I don't think we ever got there, or anywhere close."

Nicole Richie

■ *July 27*

n the early hours of Dec. 11, 2006, Nicole Richie was arrested after California Highway Patrol officers were alerted to a black Mercedes SUV headed the wrong way down Highway 134. She was booked for driving under the influence of alcohol and/or drugs after failing a field sobriety test and admitting to police that she had smoked marijuana and taken Vicodin earlier that evening. In July she was sentenced to four days in jail (she served a scant 82 minutes) and ordered to sign up for alcohol education.

Richie, 26, who was due to have a baby in January—the father is rocker Joel Madden, her beau—told Diane Sawyer during a lengthy interview that she had cleaned up her act. "No alcohol . . . no marijuana . . . no pills . . . nothing . . . no smoking around me," she said.

◼ *December 30, 2006*

THE LAST OF SADDAM

On Dec. 30—3 years, 9 months and 10 days after the U.S. invasion of Iraq—Saddam Hussein, 69, was executed by hanging, at approximately 6 a.m. Iraqi time. The former dictator was convicted, after a nine-month trial, of having ordered the massacre of Shiite Muslims in 1982.

Bootleg video footage of Hussein's execution caused a scandal.

The Year of

In 2001 he became *former* Vice President Al Gore. Instead of disappearing into a think tank, he worked doggedly on an issue he cared about. Then all of a sudden, in 2007, he was everywhere. The Oscars? There was Al (*An Inconvenient Truth*, the global-warming documentary he starred in, won two). The Live Earth concert? There was Al. Stockholm? Stunningly, Al was invited there too—to accept the Nobel Peace Prize, which he shared with the Intergovernmental Panel on Climate Change.

July 7

Gore (with Cameron Diaz, above) was instrumental in promoting Live Earth, a global megaconcert that drew 27 million viewers. Right: Giants Stadium, in East Rutherford, N.J., one of eight Live Earth venues.

AI!

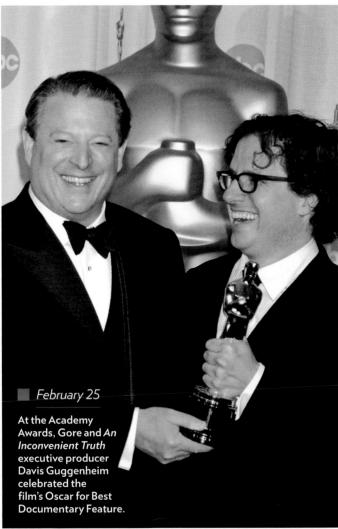

■ *February 25*

At the Academy Awards, Gore and *An Inconvenient Truth* executive producer Davis Guggenheim celebrated the film's Oscar for Best Documentary Feature.

■ *October 26*

The Nobel committee called Gore (in Spain) "probably the single individual who has done most" to warn about global warming.

Rich Pooch

When it came to her beloved Maltese Trouble, the Queen of Mean was all heart. Real estate mogul Leona Helmsley, who died Aug. 20, left $12 million of her estimated $8 billion estate for the upkeep of her 8-year-old dog, even as two of her four grandchildren got zilch, squat, diddly, nada. The canine, bought as a puppy for Helmsley by a friend, has had a colorful past: She starred in ads for Helmsley's hotels and was accused of biting a former Helmsley housekeeper, who tried and failed to sue for damages in 2005. A fan of cream cheese, steamed vegetables and grilled chicken and fish, always served by hand, the dog—and control of the pup's money—are now in the hands of Helmsley's 80-year-old brother Alvin Rosenthal.

Pets in the news

Trouble's inheritance is enough to buy 138,823 cashmere dog sweaters from Saks Fifth Avenue.

■ *October*

Iggy's Sad Tale

Talk show host Ellen DeGeneres, 49, and her partner, Portia de Rossi, 34, adopted a dog, name of Iggy, from a Pasadena animal-rescue group called Mutts and Moms. But Iggy, despite encouragement and professional training, couldn't get along with DeGeneres's three cats, so she gave the Brussels griffon mix to her hairdresser Cheryl, whose daughters Ruby, 12, and Zoe, 11, fell in love with the pup.

And then? When Mutts and Moms cofounder Marina Baktis, 38, found out about the switch, she went to Cheryl's home and—upset that she had not approved the transfer—snatched the dog, igniting a two-hour standoff involving police. Ruby watched as Baktis left with the dog. She eventually gave it to another family.

On her show DeGeneres broke down in tears talking about Iggy and her friend's daughters. "All that you're supposed to do," she said, bewildered, "is put a dog in a loving home."

OSCAR: THE CAT OF DEATH

At the Steere House Nursing and Rehabilitation Center in Providence, R.I., as patients near the end, Oscar the cat leaps on the bed, nuzzles them and purrs contentedly. Typically patients die within a few hours of his visit. "He hasn't missed one," says nurse Mary Miranda. "It just became uncanny."

Oscar, who lives in the 41-bed dementia unit, has performed his not-at-all Grim Reaper act at least 25 times; intrigued, Dr. David Dosa, who works with the Center, wrote about the feline's behavior in the *New England Journal of Medicine.* He believes Oscar's sense of smell may have something to do with his actions, but he also says the cat may be mimicking the nursing home's caregivers, who look after the dying with a ritual that includes low lights, soft music and aromatherapy. Oh do not ask for whom the cat purrs . . .

Oscar the cat has an uncanny knack for picking those soon to pass on.

O'Neal has helped his ex Farrah Fawcett cope with cancer; below, the actor with their son Redmond in December 2006.

■ *February 3*

FAMILY FIGHT

In a bizarre incident nonetheless in keeping with a troubled family history, Ryan O'Neal, 66, was arrested on assault and weapons charges. O'Neal later issued a statement claiming that, returning to his Malibu home, he walked in on a fight between his sons Griffin, 42, and Redmond, 22. Griffin, Ryan has said, swung a fireplace poker at him: "I ducked," said O'Neal. "He hit his own girlfriend in the head." The elder O'Neal said he then went to his room and retrieved a gun, which he fired into a banister as a warning when Griffin came at him with the poker. Griffin's girlfriend dialed 911, crying, "I can't see! Help me! Help me!" In May, citing insufficient evidence, the L.A. county district attorney's office dropped the charges against Ryan.

Barack the Obama Phenom

A Democratic strategist compared Obama to a "shiny red wagon: You just want to hop in and see how far it goes."

Barack Obama is far from the only Democratic presidential hopeful, but it's easy to spot his résumé among the pile: His father, who was black, was from Kenya; his mother, white and from Kansas. He grew up in Hawaii until his mother remarried, to a Muslim, and they moved to Indonesia (where Obama had an ape for a pet and the family had a transvestite cook).

Later the résumé becomes a little more like his rivals': Obama, now 46, attended Harvard Law School and became the first black president of the *Harvard Law Review,* where he became known as a consensus builder. After civil-rights work and teaching constitutional law, he was elected to the Illinois Legislature in 1996 and the U.S. Senate in 2004.

As for his presidential run, "He's in to win," said a friend who used to play dollar-ante poker with him, ". . . or he wouldn't be playing the hand."

Wilson once said he struggled with an "Irish strain of depression."

■ *August*

Owen Wilson

The world knows him as a laid-back surfer dude, whose goofy comic style and crooked nose put a lot of the quirk in such movies as *Wedding Crashers* and *Zoolander.* Then on Aug. 26, Owen Wilson, now 39, was rushed to Cedars-Sinai after slitting his wrists. Many of those who knew him were stunned— "It's impossible," said one disbelieving friend—but others said that, away from the camera, Owen was a sensitive man who'd had bouts of depression and battled drugs. "Owen is fun, kind and caring. [But] it's like he has a little John Belushi in him. He has demons."

His brothers—actors Luke, 36, and Andrew, 43—and parents rushed to his side and stayed with him around the clock. Wilson left the hospital after a few days and slowly began stepping back into normal life but, said a friend, has dropped out of movie commitments for a while. "He knows he came close to ending his life," said a friend. "He is happy that he was saved from himself."

Tom and Katie welcomed the Beckhams to the U.S. with a bash that drew a Hollywood *Who's Who*.

A trip to Toys "R" Us with (from left) sons Cruz, Brooklyn and Romeo was well documented.

Tom and Katie caught a Madrid game before Beckham moved to the U.S. to join soccer's L.A. Galaxy.

Welcome to L.A.

Give us your tired, your poor . . . and also your Brit superstars:
The Beckhams' move to America was anything but understated

Often pouty in paparazzi photos, Posh showed a lighter side—and a smile—to Jay Leno.

As part of her reality show *Coming to America*, Posh threw out the first ball at a Dodgers game.

 June

JENNIFER ANISTON

He was there . . . and then he wasn't. For one brief shining moment, Jennifer Aniston, 38, whose dating life has been at the molten core of American pop-culture ever since her 2005 break-up with Brad Pitt, was seen stepping out around L.A. with a Handsome New Guy. There they were, sharing a romantic, three-hour dinner at One Pico; a few days later they dined poolside at L.A.'s Sunset Tower Hotel. He turned out to be Brit model Paul Sculfor, 36, whom she'd met at Il Sole while dining with pal Courteney Cox. His friends gave him great reviews: "A lovely guy," said ex-girlfriend Lady Victoria Hervey. "He'll think of the woman before himself." "Quite the most ridiculously handsome man on the planet," another Sculfor pal, Clare Staples, wrote on her blog.

Alas, it may have been fun, but it was only an interlude; by summer's end there seemed to be no more dinners *à deux*.

"There's no pretense with them," said a guest at Rebecca Romijn and Jerry O'Connell's wedding. "And they're so gorgeous."

Weddings
2007

✳ **CALABASAS, CALIF.**
July 14

Rebecca Romijn & Jerry O'Connell

A MOMENT'S PAWS As actors Rebecca Romijn and Jerry O'Connell exchanged vows outside their Calabasas, Calif., home, their dog Better, dressed in a bow tie, nosed in. "He tried to jump into the ceremony," said a guest. "Rebecca started giggling, and we all laughed as he ran off."

BEYOND KARAOKE At the reception, as guests, including Romijn's *Ugly Betty* costars, sipped Perrier-Jouët, O'Connell, 33, serenaded his bride with Vanessa Williams' hit "Save the Best for Last" until Williams stepped in and belted out the final verse herself. Undeterred, the groom "did the same with a Fergie song," said a guest—until Fergie, too, grabbed the mike.

REVIEW "It was the perfect celebration," said Romijn, 34, who wore a Ralph Lauren dress. "Jerry and I couldn't be happier."

FOOTNOTE As partyers danced into the night, the newlyweds provided flip-flops for tired feet.

The wedding, said guest Vanessa Williams, was "very homespun."

Usher & Tameka Foster

SCREECH, CRASH, SOUND OF GRINDING METAL
On the morning of July 28, his scheduled wedding day, Usher called friends and family to say the nuptials were off. The sudden cancellation left in its wake stunned guests, unfinished flower arrangements and a ringing question: "Wha?!?!?!?"

WHAT WENT WRONG? Sources ascribed the 28-year-old singer's cold—nay, frozen—feet to stress from dealing with friction between his intended, Tameka Foster, 36, who was pregnant with his child, and his mother and former manager, Jonnetta Patton, 50.

FROM "ADIEU" TO "I DO"—TWICE
On Aug. 3 Usher and Tameka surprised friends again by marrying in a quiet civil ceremony in Atlanta. "Usher never intended not to marry her," said a source close to the couple. Added a friend: "When it comes down to it, she's the mother of his child. And she's a strong woman. And he loves her." His mother did not attend the ceremony. On Sept. 1 the couple married again, in front of 150 friends and family members, and danced into the wee hours.

"They were so incredibly happy. They couldn't stop smiling"

—A guest

Eva Longoria & Tony Parker

✳ **PARIS**
July 7

THE WEDDING SEASON: For the *Desperate Housewives* star, 32, and NBA player, 25, the lavish wedding (estimated cost: $1.5 million) capped a *week* of festivities that included a helicopter ride to the eighth-century medieval citadel Mont-Saint-Michel, a day trip to Disneyland Paris, an evening cruise along the Seine and an intimate civil ceremony at a Paris city hall (required to make a marriage legal in France).

THE BIG DAY: The couple treated their 250 guests—including fellow *Housewives* Teri Hatcher, Nicollette Sheridan, Felicity Huffman and Brenda Strong (Marcia Cross stayed home with her twins) to a spectacular party that didn't end until dawn. The religious ceremony took place in Paris's historic Saint-Germain-L'Auxerrois Church. Afterward guests were whisked to the 17th-century Château of Vaux-le-Vicomte, where the red-themed reception featured tens of thousands of roses, 2,000 candles and a red, five-tiered, raspberry-filled wedding cake. Fireworks lit the sky at midnight, and many guests danced until sunrise (with a 3 a.m. break for hamburgers and fries). Said *Housewives* creator Marc Cherry: "It was easily the most amazing wedding I've been to."

After exchanging Piaget bands (top), the couple and their guests danced till dawn at the Château of Vaux-le-Vicomte.

Dougray Scott & Claire Forlani

CSI: NY'S

NOT AT ALL DESPERATE: As Teri Hatcher's suitor on *Desperate Housewives*, Dougray Scott played the guy who didn't get the girl. He was more successful in real life, marrying *CSI: NY* actress Claire Forlani two years after friends introduced them.
IF YOU CAN SPELL IT YOU CAN COME: The bride's father, Pier, who is Italian, suggested they marry at a friend's estate in the small village of Pievebovigliana. "Claire went to see it," he said, "and fell in love with it."
A GREAT EXCUSE TO CATCH UP: "This is the first time they've been together in a while," said a friend. "The wedding was like a vacation for them."

PIEVEBOVIGLIANA, ITALY ✳
June 8

ONE MOMENT, PLEASE John C. McGinley felt a rush of pride as he watched his 9-year-old son Max escort his bride, Nichole Kessler, down the aisle during their intimate April 7 wedding outside their Malibu home. Then Max darted back toward the house. "I barked out orders to make sure Max was okay," recalled McGinley, 47, who plays the caustic Dr. Perry Cox on *Scrubs*. "You don't usually have the groom [yelling] at the altar, but I couldn't concentrate unless I knew Max was squared away." Turns out, Max, who has Down syndrome, was just fulfilling his best-man duties: He had gone to fetch Haley, one of the couple's two chocolate Labs, to join her mate Hudson alongside McGinley for the ceremony. Says Kessler, 34: "The sweetest thing was Max walking back with Haley, then sitting down, thinking, 'Okay, now I'm done.'"

GARAGE BAND As the reception, which included celeb pals John Cusack and John McEnroe, rolled toward dawn, the couple hosted a jam session in the garage.

MORE KIDS? "I want seven," said McGinley. Replied Nichole: "Bring it on!"

✳ **MALIBU, CALIF.**
April 7

SCRUBS'

John C. McGinley

✳ **LA JOLLA, CALIF.**
December 27

MODEL

Niki Taylor

SPEED RACER Model Niki Taylor, 31, and race car driver Burney Lamar, 26, met at a charity event in January '06 but didn't accelerate until that April, when he invited her to watch his team compete. On Sept. 15 he proposed in front of her parents. The wedding itself, at the Grande Colonial Hotel in La Jolla, Calif., on Dec. 27, had a few more witnesses: 60 friends and relatives, including Taylor's twin 12-year-old boys, Jake and Hunter, from her first marriage.

DEWY VOWS: "Everybody cried because we were all just so happy," said Taylor's rep and friend Lou Taylor (no relation). "They were really just elated, and we were all emotional."

DETAILS, DETAILS: Food? Steak, lobster and gnocchi; chocolate mousse cake. Gown? Vera Wang. Vibe? "Beautiful but very relaxed," said a guest. "That's the kind of people they are."

Hurley and Nayar in September. At the wedding, Elton John gave away the bride.

❋ GLOUCESTERSHIRE, ENGLAND
March 3

Elizabeth Hurley & Arun Nayar

THE WEDDING, PART I—CASTLE CLASSIC: Hurley and Nayar said "I do" before 300 guests at Sudeley Castle near the Cotswolds, where a row of torches lit up the pathway to the medieval estate and a local vicar did the honors. Hurley's son Damian, 4, clad in breeches, carried the rings on a purple cushion.

THE WEDDING, PART II—A PASSAGE TO INDIA: As the festivities continued—a few days and 5,200 miles away at the Umaid Bhawan Palace in Jodhpur, India— British reserve gave way to Indian splendor. There were dancing white horses, walkways lined with millions of red chili peppers and a week of parties for revelers who one night slept under tents. At the Hindu ceremony on March 9, the bride and groom circled a sacred fire as priests chanted in Sanskrit. "Liz just glowed," said Nayar's friend Arti Surendranath. "She had tears in her eyes." Before it was over, a rain shower fell from a blue sky. "It took us all by surprise," said Surendranath. "It was lovely—like a blessing from heaven."

PRIVATE PRACTICE'S

Kate Walsh

They met in February and were engaged by May. But it wasn't *only* her whirlwind romance with movie exec Alex Young that made Kate Walsh weak at the knees: Standing at the altar of the Ojai Presbyterian Church, as the temperature approached 100 degrees, the actress, 39, fainted. The ceremony was interrupted as the star of the *Grey's Anatomy* spin-off *Private Practice* was treated in a side room, but she recovered and exchanged vows with Young, 36, minutes later. By 7 p.m., said a guest, "Kate was all smiles as she greeted her guests."

✳ **OJAI, CALIF.**
September 1

NEW YORK CITY ✳
November 9

GREY'S ANATOMY'S
ELLEN POMPEO

There will be no 'big' anything," Ellen Pompeo told PEOPLE last summer about her upcoming wedding plans. "It's going to be very small."

The second of *Grey's Anatomy's* leading women to wed this year, Pompeo was true to her word. With New York City Mayor Michael Bloomberg serving as a witness, the actress and her fiancé, record producer Chris Ivery, 38, were married at City Hall in Manhattan by a clerk. Pompeo turned 38 the next day. "I'm very happy for her," said Pompeo's father, Joseph. "She just didn't want a big thing."

The couple, who met at a grocery store in 2003, were "over the moon," Pompeo's spokeswoman told *The Boston Globe*.

Roma Downey & Mark Burnett

✳ **MALIBU, CALIF.**
April 28

LOOK SHARP Having spent a lot of time with fiancé and *Survivor* creator-producer Mark Burnett, 46, Roma Downey had seen her share of jungle wear. So when it came to their wedding, the *Touched by an Angel* actress became the unofficial wardrobe mistress. "I found a beautiful gown," said Downey, 46. "Suddenly I said to Mark, 'Remember that you thought you would wear your jeans rolled up and your linen shirt? Well, you're wearing a suit.' And he just laughed and rolled his eyes."

ALL IN THE FAMILY The ceremony, in their Malibu backyard overlooking the Pacific, was a family-only affair, officiated by Downey's *Angel* costar and "adoptive mother" Della Reese, 74. Reilly, Downey's 10-year-old daughter, served as bridesmaid; Burnett's sons James, 13, and Cameron, 10, served as best man and ring bearer.

WHO'S THAT LADY? "When and if I work, I will be Roma Downey," she said. "But for everything else I will be Burnett. At this stage of my life, I really want to honor my husband. We are like teenagers in love."

Romances

High School sweethearts: Zac and Vanessa frolic on Maui in April.

✻ *April*

Zac Efron & Vanessa Hudgens

Hello, Zanessa!: For their millions of fans, the young love between Zac Efron, 20, and Vanessa Hudgens, 19, stars of the megahit TV movies *High School Musical* and *HSM2*, only added to the generation-riveting appeal of the films. At the center of it all, Efron and Hudgens kept their romance scrupulously low-profile. On the *HSM2* set, "if you didn't know they were dating, you wouldn't know they were dating," said a production source. "They're really good at not being obvious." Then they became really obvious, hugging and kissing on an April vacation together in Hawaii. "Two people fell in love," said costar Monique Coleman. "Who cares? We're good kids."

True, true. But there was that one little incident: In September a nude photo that Hudgens had taken of herself popped up on the Web. It later came to light that in 2006, after appearing on the Nickelodeon show *Drake & Josh*, Hudgens sent the images to star Drake Bell. "I want to apologize to my fans, whose support and trust means the world to me," Hudgens said in a statement that she hoped would serve as a bathrobe. "I am embarrassed over this situation and regret having ever taken these photos."

Evert and Norman (in Delray Beach, Fla.) each ended a long marriage.

Once more unto the beach: A couple on *Melrose*, the pair began dating for real this year.

✳ *September*

Greg Norman & Chris Evert

She was the biggest thing in tennis when Venus was just a planet. He was the world's best golfer before Tiger Woods went on the prowl. Now Chris Evert, 53, and Greg Norman, 52, are a couple, and each is freshly divorced. Evert's ex, former Olympic skier Andy Mill, 54, said he was blindsided when the marriage ended and his wife appeared on the arm of Norman, who had been a family friend; Norman's divorce from Laura, his wife of 25 years, involved changed locks and headlines. In early September the pair reached a settlement on how to split his estimated $400 million fortune, and Evert and Norman appeared as a couple at the U.S. Open a few days later. "We're very happy," says Evert. "We're in a good place."

So few people start dating *after* they get married, but that's the way it went for Heather Locklear and Jack Wagner. The former *Melrose Place* stars were married on that show's final episode in 1999 but didn't start seeing each other in real life until this year (Locklear, 46, split from Richie Sambora; Wagner, 48, is also recently divorced). So what's the attraction? "Jack has a great sense of humor, and we laughed at everything and still do," said Locklear. And what does Wagner like about her? "That would probably go under the category of everything," he said.

✳ *March*

Heather Locklear & Jack Wagner

Katie Couric
& Brooks Perlin

✳ *October 2006*

When CBS anchor Katie Couric chatted with Brooks Perlin, an athletic, 33-year-old entrepreneur, at a Manhattan fund-raiser in 2006, sparks didn't fly. But a mutual friend thought the two might hit it off if they just got to know each other better. "The age difference scared her off at first," another friend said of Couric, 50, who nevertheless agreed to go to dinner with Perlin a few weeks later. Things clicked, and the two have been an item ever since. "They seem comfortable with each other," says her friend. "She's a very young 50. She's playful. She's cute. She's down-to-earth. And he's mature. They seem happy." Perlin, the friend said, is "Sweet. Normal. Really grounded. It's a drama-free relationship."

The couple in New York City on May 9, 2007.

"She's crazy about him," said a friend.

✳ *August*

JENNA BUSH & HENRY HAGER

Jenna Bush, the President's daughter, dedicated her recent book *Ana's Story* to, among others, "my patient Henry." Last summer, it would seem, Henry Hager's patience was rewarded: The White House announced the couple's engagement in August. Jenna, 26, and Hager, 29, who is studying business at the University of Virginia, met while he was working for presidential advisor Karl Rove during George Bush's 2004 campaign. "Henry's very smart, very sweet—a really good guy," said Jenna's cousin, model Lauren Bush. Said Hager's dad, John, who is chairman of the Republican Party of Virginia: "We know the Bushes. We're happy, they're happy."

The roomie bargain? "I do the cooking; he cleans up," said Minnillo.

❋ April

Nick & Lachey
Vanessa Minnillo

They aren't a new couple, but they did take it up a notch: Singer Nick Lachey, 34, and former MTV *TRL* host Vanessa Minnillo, 27, moved in together, in New York City, in April. The domicile shift came less than a year after Lachey's megapublic divorce from Jessica Simpson became final in June 2006.

Even asleep, Savannah Mahoney, one of Marcia Cross's twins, seemed pretty happy about something.

"**People say, 'Oh, wait, it gets better and better!' But I'm in no rush. I'm in heaven right now**"
—Marcia Cross

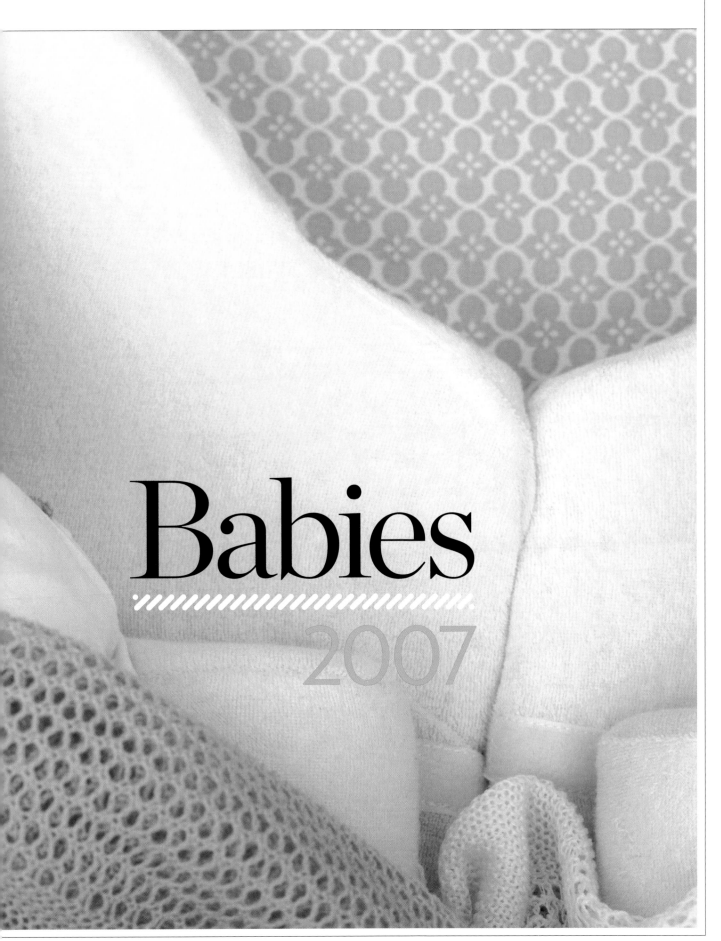

Babies

2007

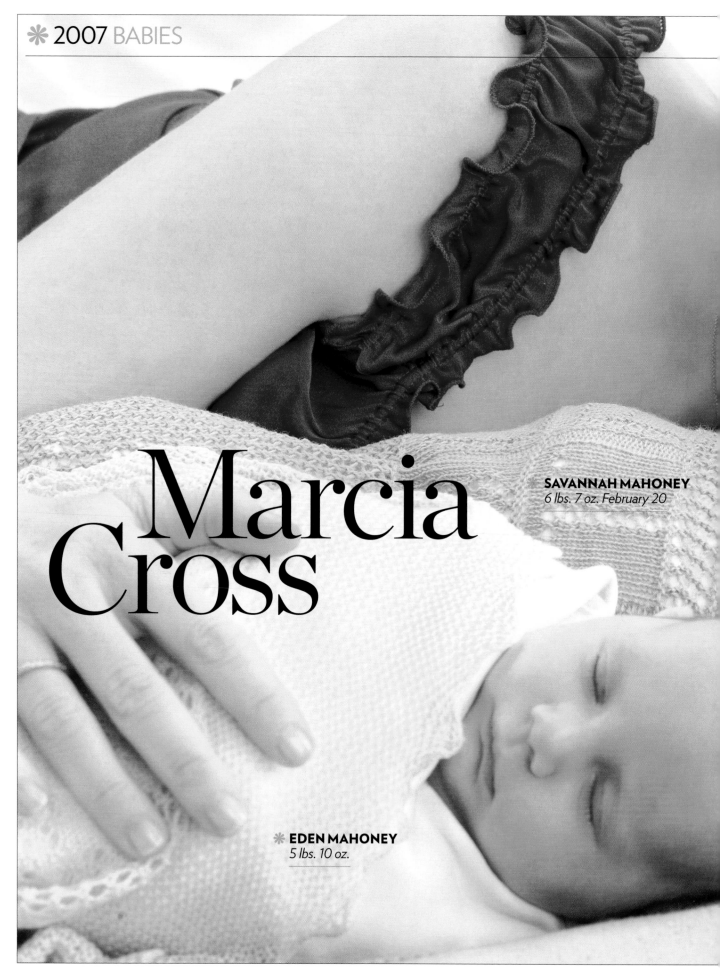

Marcia Cross

SAVANNAH MAHONEY
6 lbs. 7 oz. February 20

✻ **EDEN MAHONEY**
5 lbs. 10 oz.

> **"They're these two brand-new beings, and every day it's like, 'Who are you?'"**

"I'll tell you my routine—it's really exciting!" said *Desperate Housewives* star Marcia Cross, weeks after she and husband Tom Mahoney brought twins Eden and Savannah home from the hospital. "I feed, I burp, I change diapers, I pump. And then I have a tiny window of time to myself." Cross, who gave birth at 44, had longed for years to be a member of Club Mom. "Now I'm in and it's so much better than I even imagined," she said. "The years started going by and I was anxious about the clock ticking. Now it seems like it was all meant to be."

Inside a room in the Ho Chi Minh City Department of Justice, at about 10 a.m. on March 15, a door swung open and Angelina Jolie, 31, walked in. At that point, all eyes shifted to the boy of the hour, a quiet 3-year-old dressed in a white T-shirt, gray pants and a pair of red-frame sunglasses. After a series of document signings—Jolie was adopting the boy—the department director handed finalized paperwork to the smiling and visibly relieved Jolie. Newly named Pax Thien Jolie (now Jolie-Pitt), he joined an expanding family that includes big brother Maddox, 5 (adopted from Cambodia), and sisters Zahara, 2 (adopted from Ethiopia) and Shiloh, 9 months, the daughter born to Jolie and her partner, Brad Pitt, 43, in May 2006. Days after the adoption, a thrilled Jolie was already talking like a mother-in-awe: "You can imagine what courage it takes to be in all new surroundings, with new people and a new language," she told PEOPLE. "He is very strong."

✳ **PAX THIEN JOLIE**

Angelina Jolie

Special Double Issue

People

INSIDE OSCAR!

FIRST PHOTOS

61 PAGES OF DRESSES & DISH

PATRICK DEMPSEY'S TWINS!

AT HOME WITH THE *GREY'S ANATOMY* STAR AND HIS FAMILY

Anchor Bob Woodruff's **AMAZING RECOVERY**

MARCH 12, 2007
DISPLAY UNTIL MARCH 19, 2007
$3.99US $5.99CAN

www.people.com (AOL Keyword: People)

Patrick Dempsey with sons Darby (left) and Sullivan, born Feb. 1, 2007

DARBY GALEN DEMPSEY ✳

SULLIVAN PATRICK DEMPSEY ✳
February 1

Patrick Dempsey

As his wife, Jillian, was readied for her cesarean section, Patrick Dempsey couldn't shake the feeling that the scene was oddly familiar. "It was funny because the doctor asked if I wanted to help," said Dempsey, 41, who plays Dr. Derek Shepherd on *Grey's Anatomy*. When the twin boys were delivered, Dempsey cut the cords. Son Darby "had short, blond hair and a wider face," said Jillian, 40. "Sullivan has Sid Vicious black, punk-rock hair." Their personalities? Sullivan "is sort of the grumpy old man," said Dempsey. "Darby is very much the peaceful, quiet little Buddha." The cover story (above) was one of PEOPLE's bestsellers of 2007.

My dad gets excited by the camera: Frank with Elvis.

✱ **FRANK**
December 6, 2006

Elvis Costello & Diana Krall

Since the arrival late last year of twins Dexter and Frank, "I'm practicing the smoky, sexy, Scotch-infused tones of 'The Wheels on the Bus,'" joked jazz singer Diana Krall. Husband Elvis Costello, 52, sometimes serenades the boys on guitar, which has had one unexpected result. Now, "If we just walk into a room, they start clapping," said Krall, 42. "We didn't train them to do that for applause!"

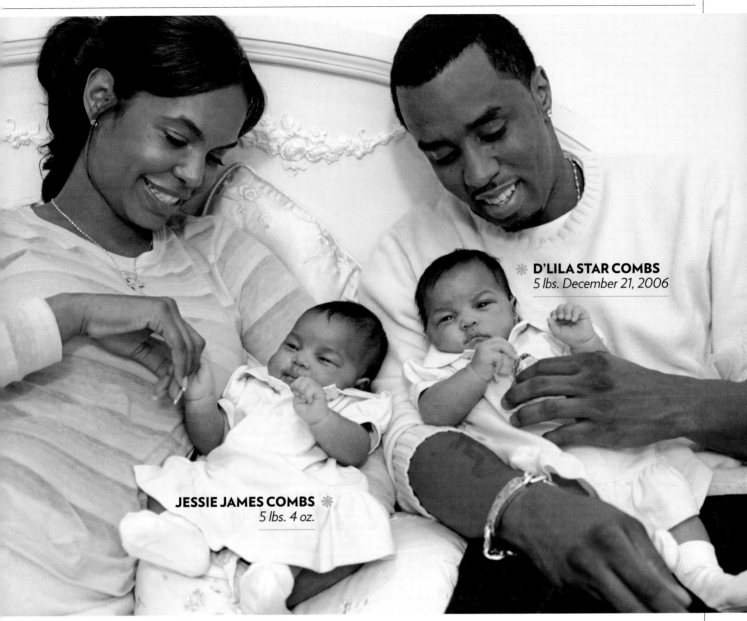

✳ **D'LILA STAR COMBS**
5 lbs. December 21, 2006

JESSIE JAMES COMBS ✳
5 lbs. 4 oz.

Diddy

A t 7 weeks old, identical twins Jessie and D'Lila Combs already had good bling. "I bought them their first pair of diamond earrings," said their dad, hip-hop and fashion mogul Sean "Diddy" Combs, 37. "Tiny Tiffany diamonds for baby girls." (No piercings until they're older, though.) Sadly, a few months later the sparkle went out of Combs' relationship with the twins' mom, longtime on-again, off-again girlfriend Kim Porter, 36; the pair split up in July.

✳ **SAM ALEXIS WOODS**
June 18

Tiger Woods

I t was quite a year for Tiger Woods, who won seven PGA Tournaments and the first-ever FedEx Cup, a series of four tournaments whose payoff was a $10 million annuity. But the highlight for Tiger was when his wife, Elin Nordegren, gave birth to their first cub, daughter Sam Alexis. "I can't describe how wonderful it is to be a father," he wrote on his Web site. "This is something I dreamed about, and I'm enjoying every minute."

Tori, husband Dean McDermott and newcomer Liam, at 5 months.

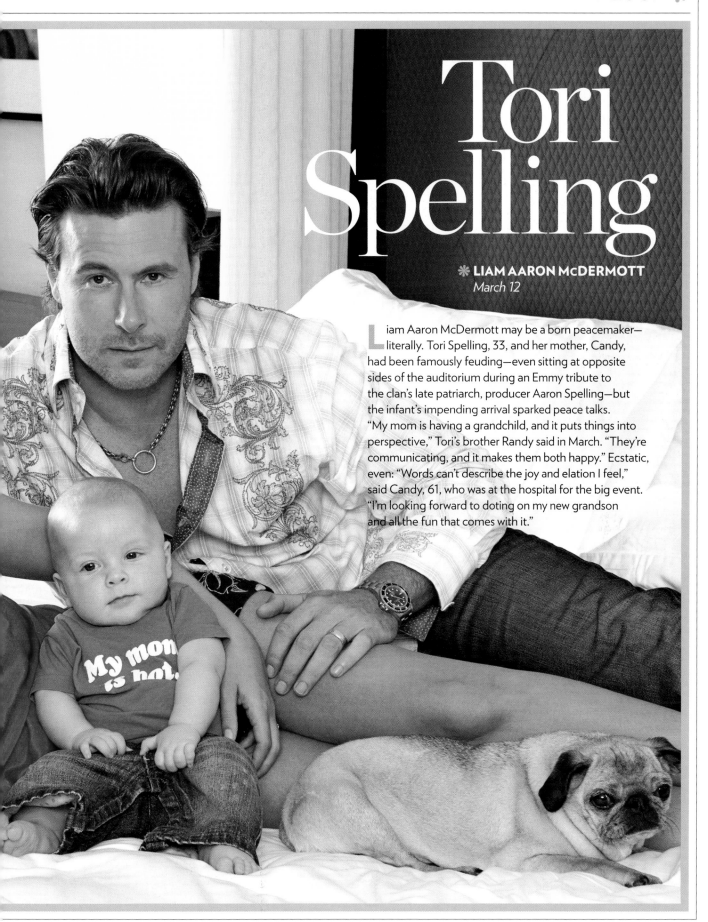

Tori Spelling

✳ **LIAM AARON McDERMOTT**
March 12

L iam Aaron McDermott may be a born peacemaker—
literally. Tori Spelling, 33, and her mother, Candy,
had been famously feuding—even sitting at opposite
sides of the auditorium during an Emmy tribute to
the clan's late patriarch, producer Aaron Spelling—but
the infant's impending arrival sparked peace talks.
"My mom is having a grandchild, and it puts things into
perspective," Tori's brother Randy said in March. "They're
communicating, and it makes them both happy." Ecstatic,
even: "Words can't describe the joy and elation I feel,"
said Candy, 61, who was at the hospital for the big event.
"I'm looking forward to doting on my new grandson
and all the fun that comes with it."

"I thought it would be like, 'Hey, you follow me,'" Eva (with Greg and George) said. "Instead, I'm following him."

✳ **GEORGE MARSIAJ HERZIG**
9 lbs. 11 oz. June 1

Eva Herzigova

Nothing like a baby to ground a jet-setting lifestyle. "Before the delivery date, my mother kept telling me, 'It's going to change your life,'" recalled model Eva Herzigova, 34. "And I was like, 'Oh, please! Four days after the delivery, I'm gonna be here, I'm gonna be there, and I'm gonna do this.'" But, after giving birth to son George, she said, "I was in the hospital—dead!"

Blame her naïveté on her too-perfect pregnancy. The model—famous for her Wonderbra billboards and currently a Chopard spokeswoman—had (hold your groans) no morning sickness and plenty of delicious cravings. "I never liked dessert before, but during the pregnancy, it was all about chocolate and whipped cream and cakes," she said. Luckily the London-based Herzigova had her boyfriend of six years, Italian businessman Gregorio Marsiaj, 31, to help stock the fridge. "I had the best support from Greg," she says.

She still does. When George wakes up during the night, Dad "puts on music and starts dancing with him," said Herzigova, adding that the boys make adorable bedfellows. "At 6 a.m. I find George in Greg's arms, remote control in his other hand, their heads down, sleeping." As for losing nearly all of the 35 lbs. she put on while pregnant, she admitted she had an unfairly svelte leg up on other new moms: "It's my DNA."

WILLIAM DYLAN O'HURLEY
7 lbs. 15 oz.
December 6, 2006

KODAK 160NC-2

54   55

John O'Hurley

He was too young to have Dad's samba steps down, but William Dylan O'Hurley quickly perfected at least one of his father's moves. "Within hours of his birth, he had my frown," said *Seinfeld* and *Dancing with the Stars* alum John O'Hurley, 53. "It begins with a furl of the eyebrows, and then they dance up and down. I said, 'It's only been five hours, and he's already got issues.'" Luckily, William—O'Hurley's first child with wife Lisa, 35—is precocious in other ways too. When the baby was just 3 months, the actor said, "He's already walking. He holds on to two of my fingers. It's like, 'Sorry, I've got places to go!'" Including the theater. O'Hurley recently moved his family to Las Vegas while he played King Arthur in *Spamalot* (where, according to one of Monty Python's best, and suddenly appropriate, lyrics, "I have to push the pram-a-lot"). "I bring him to my shows; I come to the dressing room in my king outfit with the crown on and all the gold," said the first-time dad. "You should see the look on his face."

A very green family: Fiona, Shrek and the triplets

Li'l Ogres

In *Shrek* the big guy met and married Fiona, the girl of his dreams. In the sequel *Shrek 2*, he won over his snooty in-laws. So for Summer '07's *Shrek the Third*, said director Chris Miller, "it was time to take the next step: having kids." That's kids *plural*—in fact very plural. Shrek and Fiona welcomed triplets, who were introduced to the world via a story in PEOPLE. As became clear in the movie, Shrek was ogrejoyed but, initially, overwhelmed before finding his feet as a new father. So what's next for Shrek? "Probably a midlife crisis," Miller speculated. "That's the next thing. Shrek's going to get a red Porsche."

KIM FIELDS

His bottom lip is heart-shaped—that just kills us," said Kim Fields, 37, of newborn son Sebastian, with husband Christopher Morgan, 30. Sam, as the boy is called, made his appearance after only two hours of labor. "I'm fully aware that women are jealous," Fields joked. She credits walking, yoga and sheer luck. "I don't know why God smiled on me, but I'm grateful as all get out that he did."

✳ SEBASTIAN ALEXANDER MORGAN
6 lbs. 4 oz. May 4

Donald Trump Jr.

As Donald Trump Jr., 29, posed with his very pregnant wife, Vanessa, at a New York benefit, he noted, "Being it's a Trump, I'm surprised the baby didn't want to make an appearance!" Minutes later Vanessa's water broke. The couple stuck around briefly to schmooze and raise money ("I don't know what I was thinking!" Vanessa, 29, said later) before dashing to the hospital. Twenty-one hours later Donald Sr.'s first grandchild arrived. So what should the newcomer call The Donald? "Anything," he said, "but Grandpa."

✴ **KAI MADISON TRUMP**
6 lbs. 14 oz. May 12

Life got a whole lot noisier—and more nocturnal—for Julia Roberts and her husband, cinematographer Danny Moder, this summer when they welcomed son Henry Daniel. The new guy, who tipped the scales at 8 ½ lbs., joined twin siblings Hazel and Phinnaeus, who turned 3 in November. Roberts, 39, and Moder, 38—who celebrated their fifth wedding anniversary July 4—"are really happy," said Roberts' niece (and *Nancy Drew* star) Emma, 16. "It's a good age difference with the twins." So how will Roberts juggle three kids under 4? "She is really easygoing and loving," says Emma. "She's a great mom."

HENRY DANIEL MODER *
8 lbs. 8 oz. June 18

Julia Roberts

✳ **DEZI JAMES CALVO**
6 lbs. 4 oz. May 11

Jaime Pressly

Babalooooooo II? So why did *My Name is Earl*'s Jaime Pressly, 29, and her fiancé, deejay Eric Cubiche, 32, name their newborn Dezi James? It came, said Pressly, from Cubiche's habit of calling her "Luuucy!," à la Desi Arnaz. How's the new family faring? "I used to rock all my Cabbage Patch Kids to sleep every night," said Pressly. "[Motherhood] is all I've ever wanted to do. I miss him whenever I leave the house." When she did leave the house, it was often to go to the gym: In order to fit back into her TV character's Daisy Dukes, Pressly, with her doctor's permission, started exercising only 10 days after Dezi's birth and lost most of her 40-lb. weight gain in three months.

SHERYL CROW

On May 11 Sheryl Crow announced that she had adopted a 2-week-old boy whom she named Wyatt (after her father) Steven (for her younger brother). At home in L.A., mother and son were, she said, "enjoying some very private family time." One person who could offer parenting tips? Former fiancé and father of three Lance Armstrong. "I couldn't be happier for her," the cycling champ told PEOPLE. "I know she'll be an amazing mother."

✳ **WYATT STEVEN CROW**
7 lbs. 10 oz. April 29

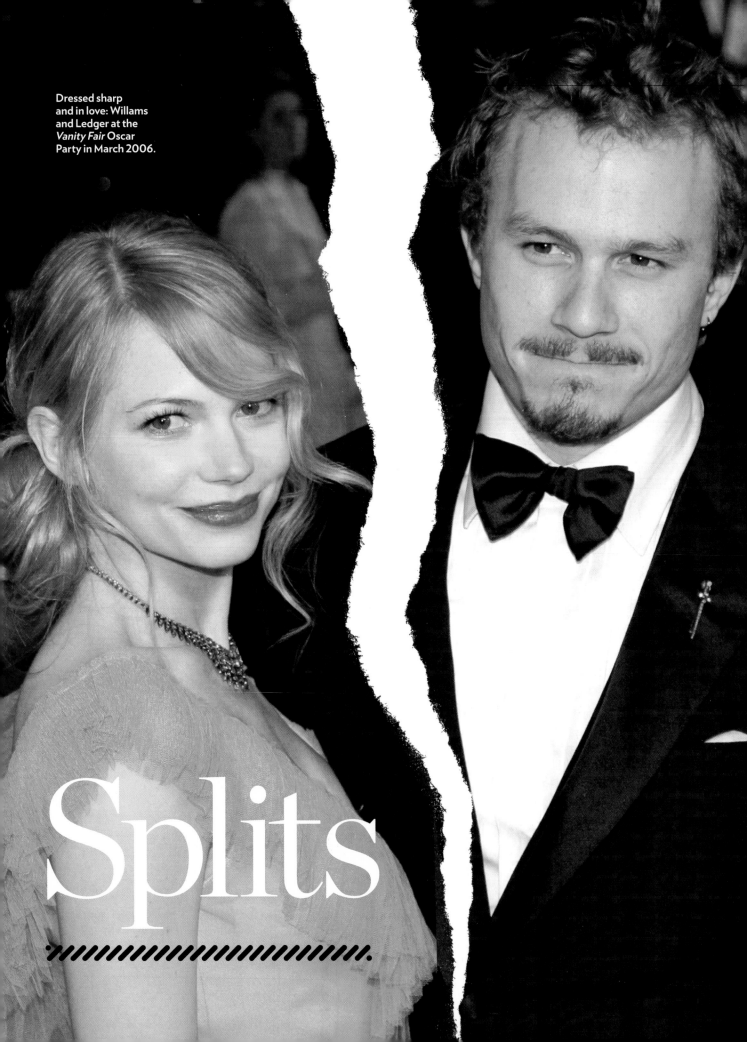

Dressed sharp and in love: Willams and Ledger at the *Vanity Fair* Oscar Party in March 2006.

Splits

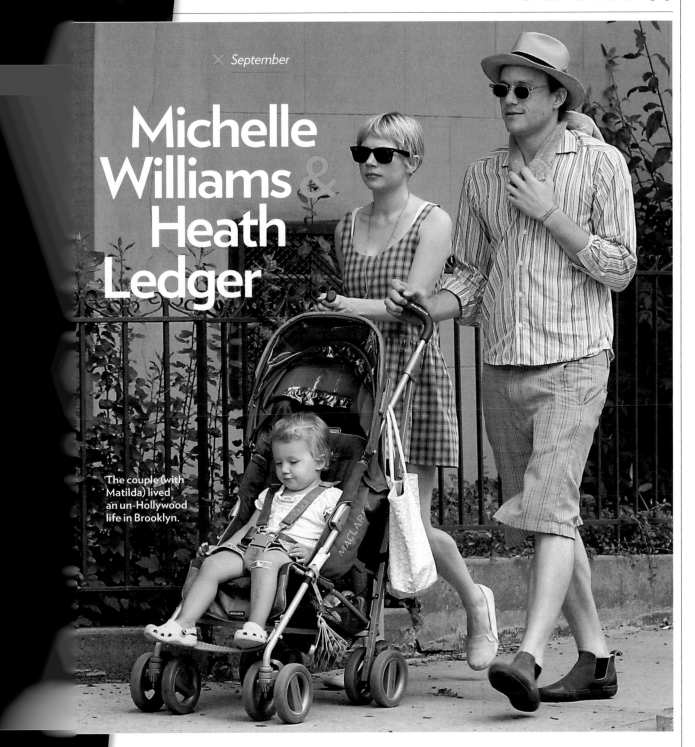

✕ *September*

Michelle Williams & Heath Ledger

The couple (with Matilda) lived an un-Hollywood life in Brooklyn.

Brokeback Mountain breakdown: Heath Ledger, 28, and Michelle Williams, 27, who met while filming the Oscar-winning story about gay cowboys, split this summer after three years and one child, Matilda, 2. "It was rocky for a while," said a source close to the couple. "They did what they could to make it work." There *had* been a fire at one time: "I remember being in rehearsal, and the two of them had googly eyes with each other," costar Jake Gyllenhaal said of the couple. The split, said the source, was amicable.

Lehmkuhl and Bass: No longer in synch.

✕ *February*

LANCE BASS & REICHEN LEHMKUHL

Former 'N Syncer Lance Bass, 28, and *Amazing Race* winner Reichen Lehmkuhl, 33, said bye, bye, bye just before Valentine's Day. The two had been partners when, partly in response to tabloid and Internet rumors, Bass went public about his sexual orientation in a PEOPLE cover story in 2006.

In one court filing, Laffoon claimed that Heche (with him in April 2006) had vandalized his shirts.

✕ *September 26*

Anne Heche & Coley Laffoon

When Anne Heche and Coley Laffoon's split became public in January, the actress's relationship with her *Men in Trees* costar James Tupper made headlines. Then the former couple turned the spotlight on each other—via a nasty divorce battle. In court papers Laffoon, 34, stated that Heche, 38, demonstrated "bizarre and delusional behavior" and questioned her ability to parent their 5-year-old son Homer. (Heche wrote about her past struggles with mental illness in her memoir *Call Me Crazy*.) The former videographer is seeking primary custody plus at least $28,000 in monthly support and $9,877 per month for a mortgage payment.

Heche fired back through her publicist, who in a statement said, "It is disappointing that Coley Laffoon has resorted to filing lies with the court because Anne would not cave in to his astronomical monetary demands.... For the past several years the child's father has refused to get a job in order to contribute financially to the child's care."

After a Sept. 26 custody hearing, both Heche and Laffoon expressed satisfaction with the result, though neither would discuss details.

"I've had my heart broken since my divorce," Simpson said in October.

✕ June 3

There was a lot of ping, and a lot of pong—and, finally, the ball just dropped off the table. "This is the 12th time they've broken up," said a source close to Jessica Simpson, referring to her June split from singer John Mayer. "Their relationship is volatile. Last week they felt better than ever. This week things are rocky. Who knows what the future will bring?" It brought . . . finality, it seems: The 12th split held. Simpson, 27, and Mayer, 30, had been dating since summer 2006.

Jessica Simpson & John Mayer

Even after the split,
Richards helped
Sambora cope with
his father's death.

✖ *March*

Denise Richards & Richie Sambora

When Denise Richards, 36, began dating Richie Sambora, 47, the ex of her onetime friend Heather Locklear, "I was called a husband stealer and a backstabber," she told *Glamour*. Still, she added, "I can't worry about being judged. Life is too short." The couple helped each other through a difficult time—Richards was also going through a divorce, from Charlie Sheen—but even tougher times contributed to the couple's split in March. Sambora's father was dying of cancer, and Richards was helping her mother battle the same disease. Friends of the couple's said that both agreed they needed to focus on their families.

✕ *April*

Paula Zahn & Richard Cohen

It was a tough year for newscaster Paula Zahn. In April tabloids reported that she and her husband of 20 years, real estate developer Richard Cohen, 59, were calling it quits. In July Zahn, 51, quit CNN the day after the network announced they'd hired a replacement. Then things got ugly: Zahn sued Cohen, demanding a detailed accounting of how he had managed her money over the years; three days later two New York City columnists reported that Cohen had found a diary in which Zahn described an affair with a married friend of theirs. "I only know Paula casually," says someone in her social circle. "But man, oh man, this is one horrible mess."

"Our family will pull together," said Judd, a mom, after splitting from Roach (left).

Very quickly Cohen and Zahn (in 2000) began lobbing charge and countercharge.

✕ *March 27*

WYNONNA JUDD & DAN ROACH

At their 2003 wedding, they danced to "Over the Rainbow." Four years later a very dark cloud set in: Country star Wynonna Judd's husband, Dan Roach, 50, was arrested and later indicted on three counts of aggravated sexual battery against a minor under 13. Judd, 42, immediately filed for divorce. "I am obviously devastated," said the singer.

So much more fun than SAT prep: Zac (in blue shirt), Vanessa (to his left) and the gang.

High School Musical 2

+ FROM SLEEPER TO MONSTER

Television

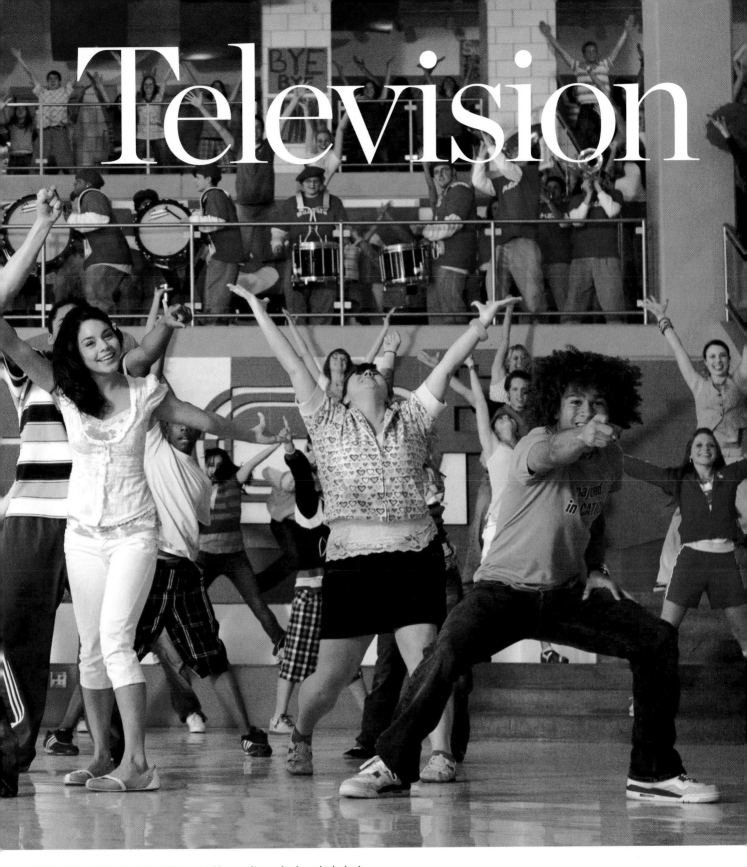

High School Musical, the Disney's Channel's perky hey-kids-let's-put-on-a show extravaganza, was a surprise hit in January 2006; the sequel, which aired for the first time on Aug. 17, garnered the biggest audience in basic-cable history. The *HSM* pack, Corbin, Ashley, Vanessa and Zac, will likely be back next year, in cinemas.

✚ FOLLICULAR FAD

American Idol

Sanjaya Malakar, the *American Idol* Season 6 contestant and mascot, rocked the ponyhawk-seen-round-the-world and other creations. What was the Seattle 18-year-old like before he amassed an army of Fanjayas? "I'm just quirky," he admitted. "I'm a weird person, but it's cool. If there weren't weird people, the world would be boring." Nothing, it seems, can dim that impish grin—not even judge Simon Cowell's savagery. Behind Cowell's bluster, said Sanjaya, "is a shiny, happy person."

This week in hair: Four faces of Sanjaya. He also danced the hula.

Whitney, Lauren, Audrina and Heidi: *The Hills* are alive with the sound of gossip.

The Hills

BLONDE VS. BLONDE

Heidi and Lauren were friends, then Heidi began dating Spencer, but Lauren said Spencer was icky, and Spencer and Heidi urged Lauren's friend Jen to get together with Brody, Lauren's ex, and then there was a rumor that Lauren had made a sex tape, and Lauren blamed Heidi and Spencer, so now Lauren Conrad, 21, and Heidi Montag, 21, stars of the reality-TV series *The Hills,* are on the outs, and Heidi and Spencer Pratt, 24, an Eddie Haskell for the New Millennium, are engaged. Reconciliation? "Not going to happen," said a Lauren loyalist.

The Sopranos

+ GUINNESS RECORD FOR MAKING THE MOST
PEOPLE GO "WHA????"

Chrissy's dead, Silvio's on life support, and Big Pussy sleeps with the
fishes. And in the breathlessly anticipated last moments of HBO's awards
juggernaut *The Sopranos* (six seasons, 21 Emmys), mob boss Tony Soprano
is . . . listening to Journey on the jukebox and about to order dinner in a
diner with his family? (But wait . . . who's that guy sitting at the counter?)

+ LITTLE BIG GIRL

Hannah Montana

If you don't know her, there are not enough 10-year-olds in your life. Miley Cyrus's TV show *Hannah Montana,* about an average kid who lives a double life as a pop star, is a huge hit; her most recent release, *Hannah Montana 2/Meet Miley Cyrus,* topped *Billboard*'s album chart, making her the youngest solo female to have a No. 1 album, and tickets to her tour were reportedly scalped for $2,000. The biggest challenge, says her dad, country star Billy Ray Cyrus, is maintaining a normal home life for his 14-year-old daughter. "I pray every day," he said, "she can stay on that path."

+ THE NEWCOMER

30 Rock

Tight scripts, Alec Baldwin and an unhackneyed approach to comedy made *30 Rock,* Saturday Night Live veteran Tina Fey's send-up of backstage life at an *SNL*-type show, a hit. "Hilarious," "sly," "savvy" and "bliss," said critics; Emmy voters settled for calling it the Outstanding Comedy Series.

Sil gets shot, Paulie gets a job he doesn't want, and Tony gets . . . dinner?

Rock stars: Alec Baldwin, Tina Fey and Tracy Morgan.

Movies

Son, someday you'll have abs like these: Gerard Butler says his goodbyes before battle.

Pirates, Shrek, Bourne

✚ IF AT FIRST YOU SUCCEED, TRY, TRY AGAIN

Three of the biggest 2007 movies were sequels to sequels: *Pirates of the Caribbean: At World's End* minted lucre; *Shrek the Third* took a look at how the jolly-but-beleaguered green giant and Princess Fiona raised triplets; and *The Bourne Ultimatum* cemented star Matt Damon's status as a Hollywood Big Gun.

PIRATES III

SHREK III

AND THE SPARTAN DESIGN AWARD GOES TO . . .

300

Director Zack Snyder's highly stylized, hyperviolent comic-come-to-life retelling of the battle of Thermopylae (where, according to legend, a small band of Spartans, fighting to the last man, held off a massive Persian invasion in 480 B.C.) was mocked by some critics, but his ripped, buffed, barely clothed little-army-that-could slew the mighty god Box Office and brought back a treasure worth over 400 million.

+ NERDS RULE

Knocked Up & Superbad

Knocked Up, a rollicking film about the hilarity that ensues after a one-night stand leads to an unexpected pregnancy, was one of the year's highest-grossing comedies ($148 million). Costar Jonah Hill, who appeared in *Knocked Up* and the summer's other gross-out hit, *Superbad,* was thus catapulted into, if not stardom, mid-level recognizability.

BOURNE III

The Police

Twenty-three years after they last toured, Sting, Andy Summers and Stewart Copeland reunited to sing "Roxanne" and other classics.

Music

You don't have to turn on the red light: the Police in L.A. in June.

KATHARINE McPHEE

CHRIS DAUGHTRY

TAYLOR HICKS

✚ BIG WIN

American Idol

Taylor Hicks won *American Idol*, and Katharine McPhee was the runner-up. But when the Season 5 competitors released their albums, the winner at the cash register was ... rocker Chris Daughtry, who had finished fourth. According to Nielsen SoundScan, by November 2007 *Katharine McPhee* had sold 360,000 copies; *Taylor Hicks* 697,000; and Daughtry's *Daughtry* 3.3 million.

✚ BIG STAR

Carrie Underwood

And speaking of *Idol*: Season 4's Carrie Underwood won two Grammys in 2007, and her album *Some Hearts*, with more than 6 million sold, passed Kelly Clarkson's *Breakaway* to become the bestselling album by an *Idol* winner.

Amy Winehouse

✛ BIG TROUBLE

By year's end tough-chick Brit singing sensation Amy Winehouse, 24—whose second album, *Back to Black*, debuted at No. 7 on *Billboard*'s U.S. album chart—was making more news for her personal life than for her jazz- and girl-group-influenced music. In May she surprised family and fans by marrying former boyfriend Blake Fielder-Civil, 25; in August the two checked in to rehab together but left after five days. In the ensuing months, the singer, who is said to have battled bulimia in the past, canceled various concerts claiming illness or fatigue, was photographed looking bloody and bruised on the streets of London and arrested for marijuana possession in Norway. (Separately, in November, Fielder-Civil was arrested in a case that involved the beating of a bartender; he's denied the charges.)

In late August Winehouse's father-in-law, Giles Civil, alarmed at the couple's increasing troubles, proposed that fans boycott her music in an attempt to get her to change her life.

Winehouse's hits include "Rehab;" her DVD is called *I Told You I Was Trouble*.

✛ BIG BEEF

Kanye West & 50 Cent

Rihanna, Fergie and Stefani: Leaders in their field.

BY THE NUMBERS

+ The most-downloaded songs of 2007 through mid-November, according to Nielsen SoundScan

2.2 million
FERGIE "BIG GIRLS DON'T CRY"
BESTSELLING SONG

2.1 million
GWEN STEFANI "THE SWEET ESCAPE"
BESTSELLING ALTERNATIVE
ROCK TRACK

2.1 million
SOULJA BOY TELL'EM
"CRANK THAT (SOULJA BOY)"
BESTSELLING HIP HOP TRACK

1.7 million
PLAIN WHITE T'S "HEY THERE DELILAH"
BESTSELLING ROCK SONG

1.4 million
CARRIE UNDERWOOD
"BEFORE HE CHEATS"
BESTSELLING COUNTRY SONG

1.4 million
RIHANNA "UMBRELLA"
BESTSELLING R&B SONG

In a much-hyped "feud" that would make a wrestling promoter proud, Kanye West (above, right) and 50 Cent traded boasts about whose new album would sell more during the first week, with 50 promising he would "not put out any new solo albums" if he lost. West won . . . but 50 quickly backtracked, saying his album beat Kanye in Europe. (Does that mean 50 will have to confine himself to recording in Luxembourg?) Meanwhile, Nielsen SoundScan numbers suggested that, for 2007, Miley Cyrus might stomp them both, or come close.

Best & Worst

Down the red carpets they came, draped, wrapped, stitched, pinned and, perhaps, even taped into Dolce, Versace, Cavalli and Kors. Who made viewers go "mmmmm," and who made viewers go "hmmmmm..."?

+ REESE WITHERSPOON
In Nina Ricci at the Academy Awards
February 25

BEYONCE
KNOWLES
Armani Privé

CATE
BLANCHETT
Armani Privé

JENNIFER
LOPEZ
Marchesa

February 25

The Academy Awards

///////////////////////////////

PENELOPE
CRUZ
Atelier Versace

NICOLE
KIDMAN
Balenciaga by Nicolas Ghesquiere

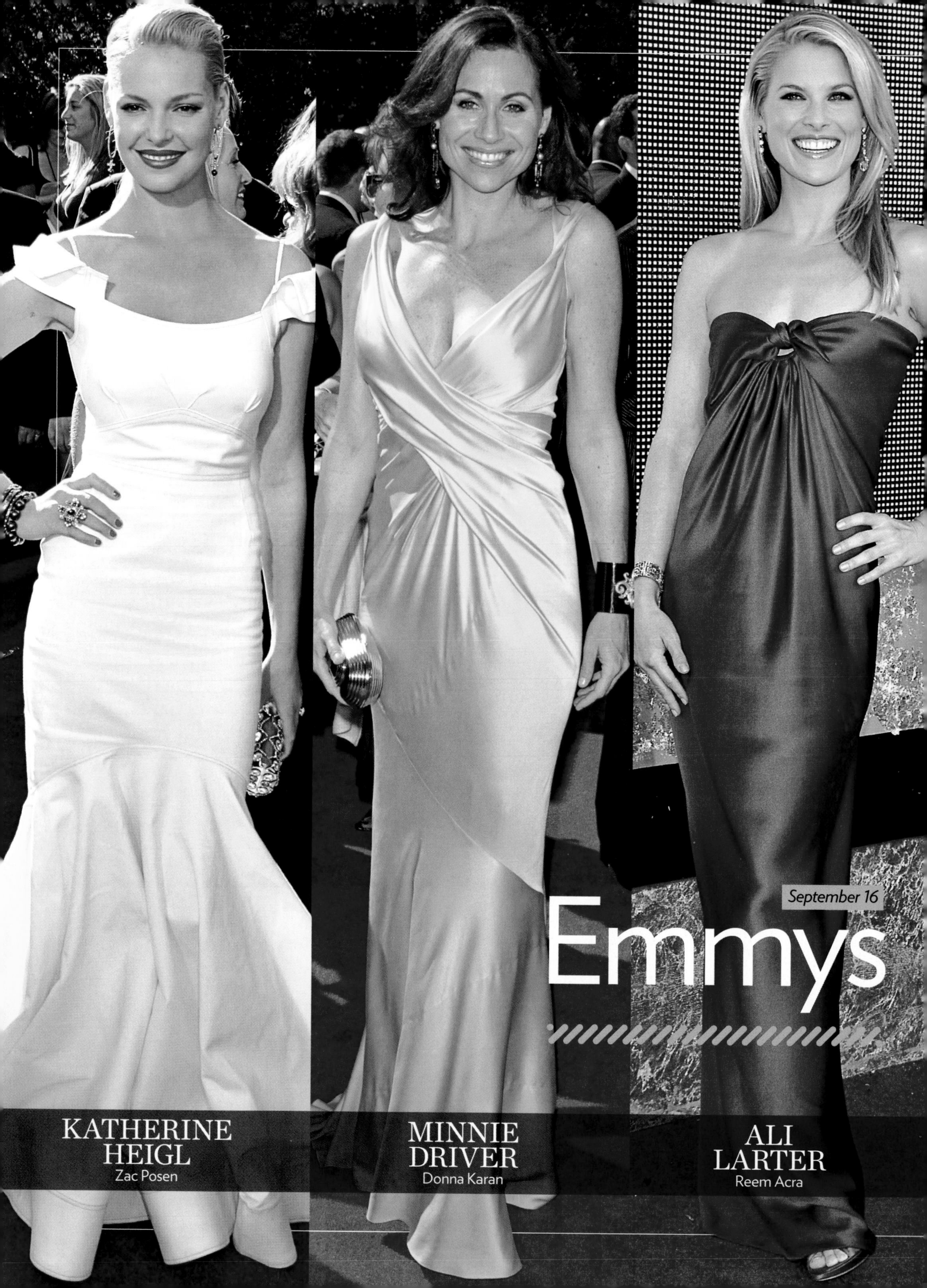

September 16

Emmys

KATHERINE
HEIGL
Zac Posen

MINNIE
DRIVER
Donna Karan

ALI
LARTER
Reem Acra

EVA
LONGORIA
KaufmanFranco

AMERICA
FERRERA
Monique Lhuillier

DEBRA
MESSING
Ralph Lauren

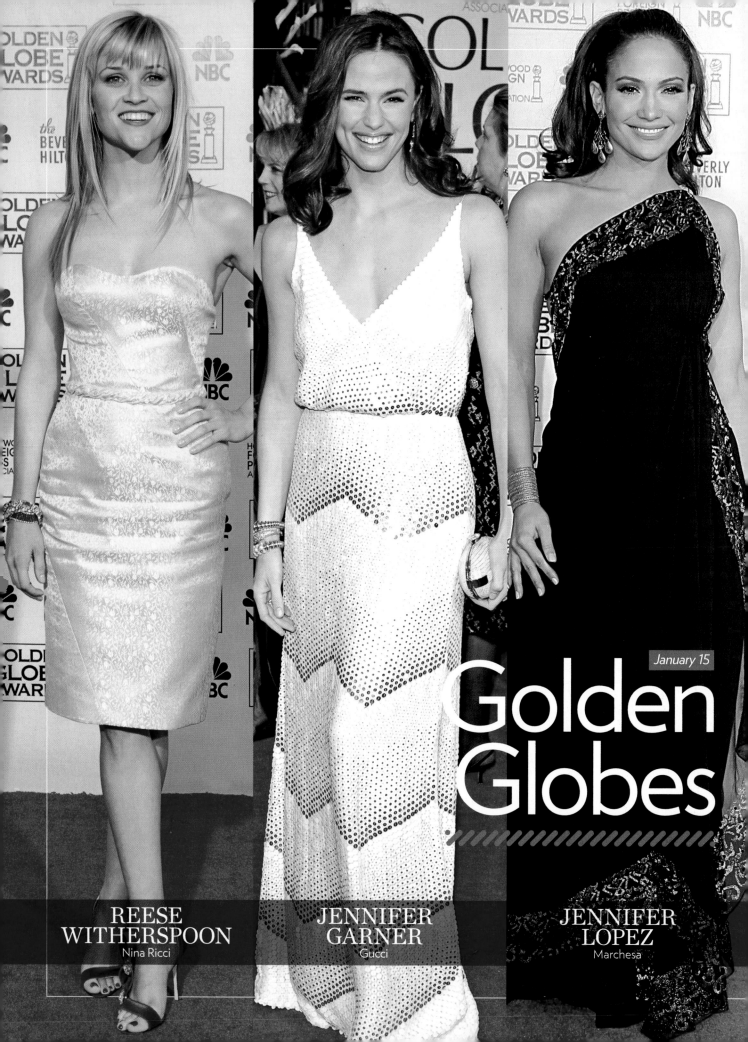

January 15

Golden Globes

REESE
WITHERSPOON
Nina Ricci

JENNIFER
GARNER
Gucci

JENNIFER
LOPEZ
Marchesa

DREW BARRYMORE
Dior Haute Couture by John Galliano

CAMERON DIAZ
Valentino

NAOMI WATTS
Gucci

January 28

SAGs

ANNE
HATHAWAY
Marchesa

JOY
BRYANT
Valentino

ELLEN
POMPEO
Lanvin

DEMI MOORE
Alberta Ferretti

CATE BLANCHETT
Giorgio Armani

AMERICA FERRERA
Badgley Mischka

ANGELINA JOLIE
Emanuel Ungaro
The premiere of *Ocean's Thirteen* in Cannes

CAMERON DIAZ
Dior by John Galliano
Met Costume Institute Gala in N.Y.C.

KERRY WASHINGTON
Oscar de la Renta
The premiere of *I Think I Love My Wife* in Hollywood

The Best of the Rest

KATE BOSWORTH
Prada
Met Costume Institute Gala in N.Y.C.

DREW BARRYMORE
Versace
Rodeo Drive Walk of Style
in Beverly Hills

EVA MENDES
Valentino
Valentino's 45th Anniversary
Gala Ball in Rome

KIRSTEN DUNST
"I don't know. It just nested there."

RINKO KIKUCHI
The world's tallest toy poodle?

QUEEN LATIFAH
Auditions for *The Golden Girls*.

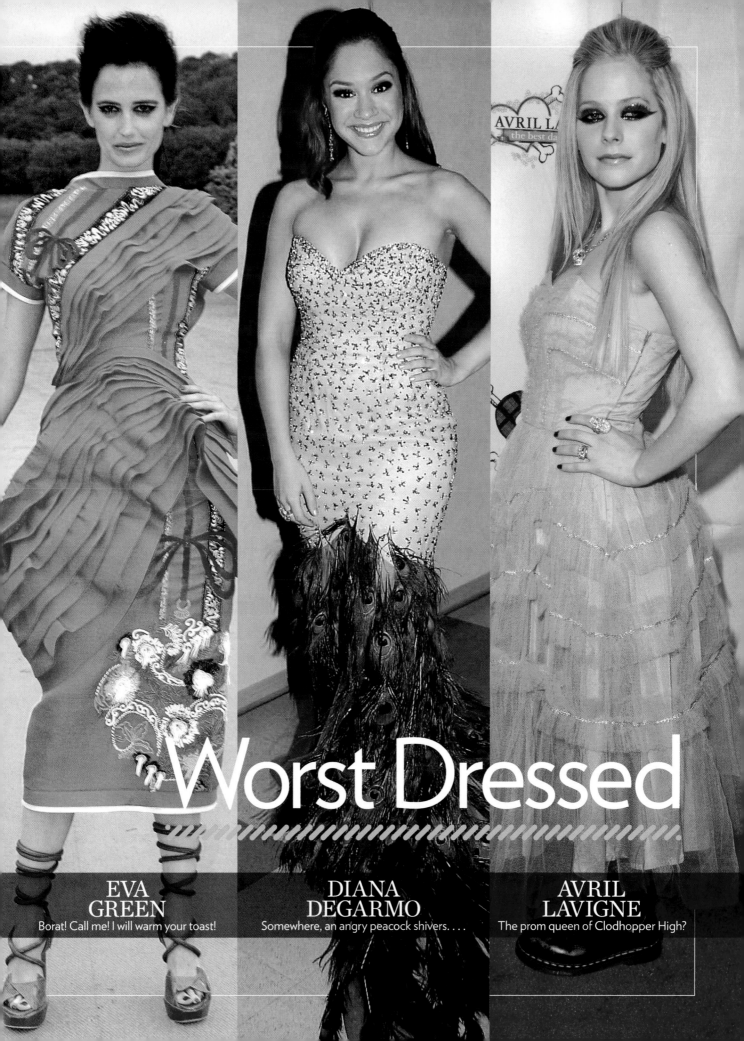

Worst Dressed

EVA GREEN
Borat! Call me! I will warm your toast!

DIANA DEGARMO
Somewhere, an angry peacock shivers. . . .

AVRIL LAVIGNE
The prom queen of Clodhopper High?

That's so
2007

Like sand through an hourglass, so are the fashion trends of our times. This was *your* year, white sunglasses!

THE RAZORED BOB
What about bobs? The highly attitudinal, shorter dos were hair, there and everywhere, including Jenny McCarthy, Victoria Beckham and Rihanna.

GIANT WHITE SUNGLASSES!
For slightly longer than a camera flash, white-framed shades were 2007's signature celeb accessory (from left: Paris Hilton, Drew Barrymore).

WIDE-LEG PANTS
Muffin tops, be gone! Roomier jeans began to make headway (Katie Holmes).

FEDORA
An old-is-new look that said leave the gun, take the cannoli . . . and who's up for a cosmo? (Jessica Alba)

TENT DRESS
More dessert? Why not! Under the big top, nobody knows! (Eva Mendes)

YELLOW
In the summer of 2007, bright yellow (Kate Hudson) had its moment in the sun.

GLADIATOR SANDALS
Mary-Kate Olsen wore an extra-high pair; they caught on with roamin' legions.

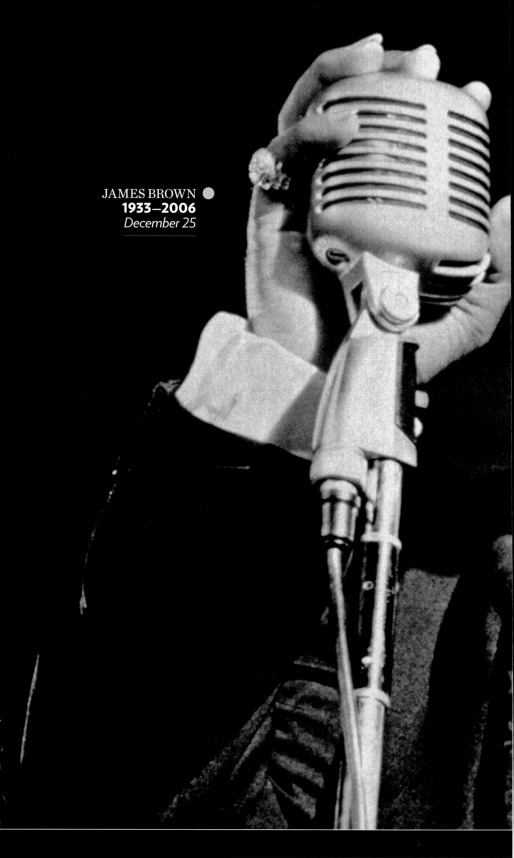

JAMES BROWN ●
1933–2006
December 25

The classic years: James Brown
at Harlem's Apollo Theater
sometime in the early '60s.
Typically, at the end of each show,
an emcee would throw a cape
over an "exhausted" Brown, who
would then stagger toward the
wings—only to throw off the
cape and, somehow, summon
the strength for an encore.

Obituaries

2007

"I feel good,
I knew that
I would"
—James Brown,
"I Got You (I Feel Good)"

Get on up: The man who
sang "A woman gotta
use what she got/ To
get just what she wants"
took a flying leap on
Broadway in 1979.

James Brown

Elvis was the King, but James Brown was the Godfather of Soul, Soul Brother No. 1 and, of course, the Hardest Working Man in Show Business. Raised in poverty, he served time in jail for breaking into cars before scoring his first hit, "Please, Please, Please," in 1956. For decades afterward he produced a yowling, rhythm-heavy sound whose titles—"I Got You (I Feel Good)," "Papa's Got a Brand New Bag," "Get Up Offa That Thing," "Say It Loud—I'm Black and I'm Proud," "Give It Up or Turn It Loose," "Hot Pants"—often comprised most of the lyrics as well.

His personal life frequently made headlines: Brown was married four times and had at least six children. In 1988 police who were chasing him had to shoot out the tires of his truck, and he spent 15 months in jail on assault charges. The Hardest Working Man in Show Business stopped working at 73, after a long battle with pneumonia. His inimitable musical legacy—only James Brown sounds like James Brown—will continue to be a mother lode for music samplers for decades. Said Island Def Jam Music Group chairman L.A. Reid: "James Brown has influenced black music more than any other entertainer, dead or alive."

In Rome, Soul Brother No. 1 and his then wife, Adrienne, met Pope John Paul II.

In 1968 the Hardest Working Man in Show Business took his act to Vietnam.

"I am acutely aware that you have not elected me . . . by your ballots. So I ask you to confirm me with your prayers"

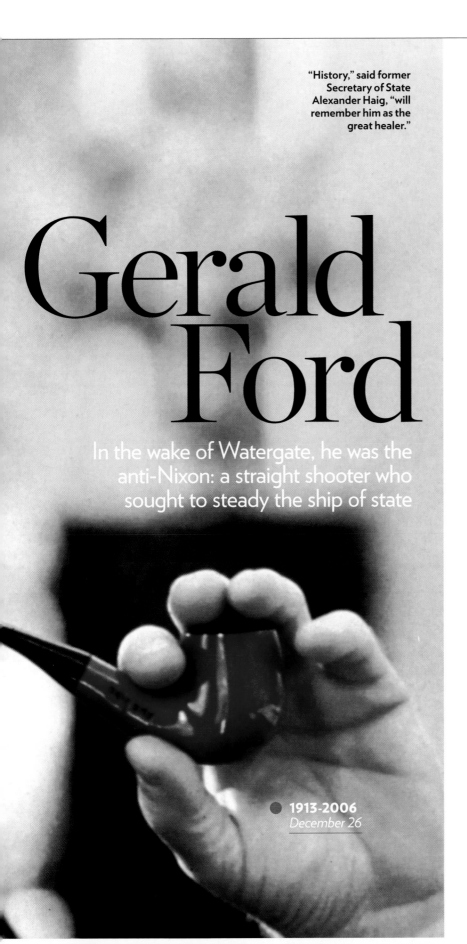

"History," said former Secretary of State Alexander Haig, "will remember him as the great healer."

Gerald Ford

In the wake of Watergate, he was the anti-Nixon: a straight shooter who sought to steady the ship of state

● **1913-2006**
December 26

After taking the oath of office as President on Aug. 9, 1974, the day Richard Nixon, battered by the Watergate scandal, resigned in disgrace, Gerald Ford told a shaken nation, "I have not sought this enormous responsibility, but I will not shirk it."

A former college football star and 12-term Michigan congressman, Ford, who died at age 93 after battling heart disease, proved himself a deft and amiable President. "Ford listened to people in a way that was exceptional," says Stephen Hess, a public affairs professor at George Washington University. "He truly had an open mind."

Thirty days into the job, Ford pardoned Nixon, which he insisted was essential to lay the Watergate ordeal to rest. That act ignited charges that Ford had agreed to let his former boss off the hook even before taking office. Years later, Ford observed, "I should have said that acceptance of a pardon by Mr. Nixon was an admission of [his] guilt."

A wily politician with a battering-ram style, Yeltsin tried to lead Russia through the chaos of the Soviet Union's collapse.

● **1931–2007**
April 23

Boris Yeltsin

From the moment he scrambled atop a tank to rally Muscovites against a coup in 1991, it was clear Boris Nikolayevich Yeltsin knew how to seize the day. As Russia's first freely elected leader in 1,000 years, the burly Siberian relied on his bold personality. "I remember one time going with him into the Kremlin," a German journalist recalled. "As he whizzed past the secretaries, he poked them in the ribs like a naughty boy."

Yeltsin, who died at 76 of heart failure, drove Russia's chaotic transformation into a fledgling democracy, but public opinion eventually turned against him after crime flourished and tycoons hijacked state assets. He resigned in 1999. "Fate gave him a tough time in which to govern," said Bill Clinton, "but history will be kind to him."

Famous for her mascara, Messner also became known, later on, for compassion.

● **1942–2007**
July 20

TAMMY FAYE

Tammy Faye Messner gained national fame when her then-husband, Rev. Jim Bakker, was caught embezzling millions. Resilient, she remarried and reinvented herself. Messner embraced gays, hosted a talk show and appeared on *The Surreal Life* with, among others, porn icon Ron Jeremy. "She stood up for all kinds of people," said Jeremy, who became a friend.

On July 20 Messner, 65, appeared on *Larry King Live* to talk about her battle with cancer. Hours later, she died.

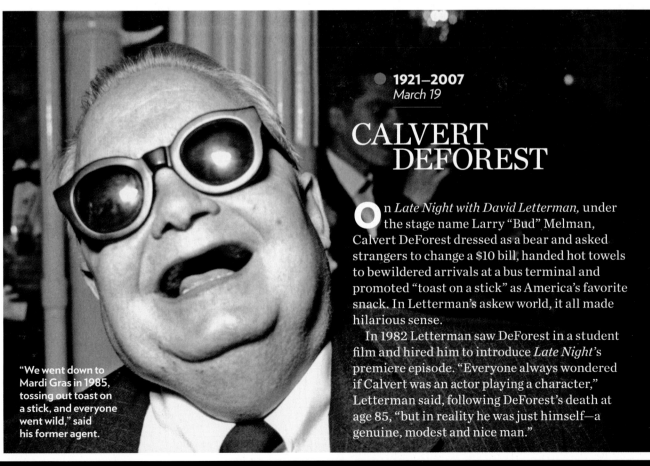

"We went down to Mardi Gras in 1985, tossing out toast on a stick, and everyone went wild," said his former agent.

● **1921–2007**
March 19

CALVERT DEFOREST

On *Late Night with David Letterman,* under the stage name Larry "Bud" Melman, Calvert DeForest dressed as a bear and asked strangers to change a $10 bill, handed hot towels to bewildered arrivals at a bus terminal and promoted "toast on a stick" as America's favorite snack. In Letterman's askew world, it all made hilarious sense.

In 1982 Letterman saw DeForest in a student film and hired him to introduce *Late Night*'s premiere episode. "Everyone always wondered if Calvert was an actor playing a character," Letterman said, following DeForest's death at age 85, "but in reality he was just himself—a genuine, modest and nice man."

> ❝ [*The Munsters*] made me hot again, which I wasn't for a while❞ —De Carlo

● **1922–2007**
January 8

Yvonne De Carlo

She dressed like the walking dead on the '60s sitcom *The Munsters*, but Yvonne De Carlo carried herself like a star: "When she walked into a room," said Butch Patrick, who played her werewolfish son Eddie, "everybody knew it."

Her Old Hollywood glamour was the real thing. In the '40s and '50s, De Carlo, who died at 84, honed her sultry screen presence in B movies opposite the likes of Burt Lancaster (in 1949's *Criss Cross*) and Rock Hudson (1953's *Sea Devils*); she played Mrs. Moses in *The Ten Commandments*. Offscreen she dated Lancaster, Jimmy Stewart and Howard Hughes.

Her icy TV pallor hid a warm heart: "She was sweet and kind," said Patrick. "A good TV mother."

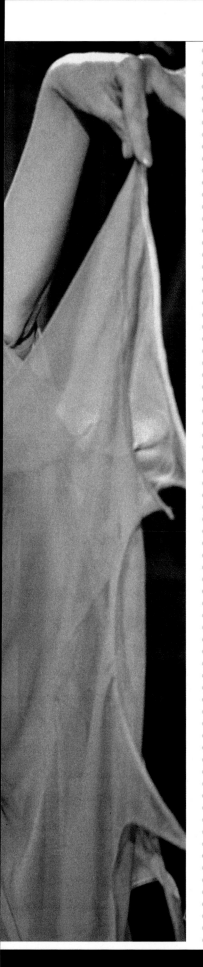

1935–2006
December 12

Peter Boyle

Over 40 years he appeared in everything from *Taxi Driver* to *Monster's Ball* to *Scooby-Doo 2: Monsters Unleashed*. Offscreen Peter Boyle, who died at 71 of heart disease and multiple myeloma, studied with Uta Hagen, was an antiwar activist in the '70s and had a wide and unusual circle of friends (John Lennon was best man at his 1977 wedding). He will probably be best remembered as the tap-dancing monster in Mel Brooks's *Young Frankenstein* and for his nine seasons playing Ray Romano's dad on *Everybody Loves Raymond*. "He became a mentor," Romano told ENTERTAINMENT WEEKLY, "and as neurotic as I am, as much as I hate myself, I can honestly say I felt his friendship."

1902–2007
August 13

Brooke Astor

Her father-in-law, capitalist John Jacob Astor IV, died on the *Titanic*; when her husband, Vincent Astor, died in 1959, Brooke Astor inherited a fortune. Over the next four decades, the Grand Dame of New York high society dedicated herself—between museum openings and visits to the zoo—to giving much of her fortune away: By the time of her death, at 105, she had donated some $200 million to institutions benefiting New York culture, schools and housing.

In 2006 Astor's grandson Philip Marshall accused his own father, Anthony, of misusing her money. Marshall denied the charges but agreed to stop managing his mother's affairs. A battle is already underway over Astor's estate, valued at about $190 million.

1931–2007
May 25

Charles Nelson Reilly

Armed with a wicked wit and a collection of ascots, Charles Nelson Reilly was a fixture on '70s TV—schmoozing with Johnny Carson (he appeared nearly 100 times) and trading bons mots on *The Match Game*. The TV quipmeister also had a more serious side: He won a Tony Award in 1962 for his performance in *How to Succeed in Business Without Really Trying* and was nominated two more times, once in 1964 for *Hello, Dolly!* and again in 1997 for directing a revival of *The Gin Game*. Notably, Reilly was also openly gay in Hollywood long before many others took the leap. "He was flamboyant at a time [when] that was far ahead of the curve," said a close friend. "He allowed people to feel better about themselves."

Luciano Pavarotti

1935–2007 ●
September 6

Indisputably the biggest and most beloved opera star of his time, Luciano Pavarotti serenaded the world for 45 years. With one of opera's most beautiful voices—bright, sensual and infused with joy—he created a style that was his alone.

But highbrow fame was only part of his dream: His Three Tenors collaborations with Placido Domingo and José Carreras sold millions. At his Pavarotti & Friends charity concerts, he sang duets with Sting and Bono. Purists scoffed at his commercial pursuits, but Pavarotti, who died of pancreatic cancer at 71, told PEOPLE, "These are things that will bring this little world of opera to a larger audience, and I don't care how we do it."

Even at 76, Don Ho was a Hawaiian icon. At the Ohana Waikiki Beachcomber hotel in Honolulu, Ho sang island tunes, welcomed out-of-towners and closed his show with a second performance of his signature hit "Tiny Bubbles," often jokingly dedicated to "those of us who can't remember if I sang it earlier." As usual, on April 12 he got a standing ovation.

It would be his last. Two days later Ho died of heart failure. Thousands attended a May 5 memorial, after which a flotilla of canoes carried the singer's ashes out to sea. "He knew how famous he was, but he could never understand it," said a friend. "I imagine right now he's looking down and thinking, 'Wow.'"

● 1930–2007
April 14

Don Ho

He was, perhaps, best known to the public as a talk show host, but few in Hollywood possessed Merv Griffin's astounding breadth of talents. He played piano at 4 and was fronting a big band at 19; his first big hit was "I've Got a Lovely Bunch of Coconuts." For 23 years, as the host of *The Merv Griffin Show*, he chatted with everyone who mattered, from President Ronald Reagan and Dr. Martin Luther King Jr. to Richard Burton,

Jane Fonda and John Lennon. He created the game shows *Jeopardy!* and *Wheel of Fortune*, built a gambling and real-estate empire and was worth more than $1 billion.

Griffin, who died of prostate cancer at 82, always gave the impression that he enjoyed the journey as much as the destination. "[My father] was like the Energizer Bunny," said his son Tony. "This wasn't his type of ending. He's a guy who just gets up and has fun and entertains."

● **1925–2007**
August 12

Merv Griffin

1947 BLACK NARCISSUS

1953 FROM HERE TO ETERNITY

1956 THE KING AND I

1957 AN AFFAIR TO REMEMBER

Kerr was known for her genteel English demeanor until she unleashed her sultry side in *From Here to Eternity*. Among other memorable roles, she starred with Yul Brynner in *The King and I* and Cary Grant in *An Affair to Remember* before leaving Hollywood, at age 48, saying she was "either too young or too old" for the roles being offered.

1921–2007
October 16

Deborah Kerr

Few people will remember that she was nominated for six Oscars but never won, but movie fans of almost any age won't forget her most famous scene: locking lips on the beach with Burt Lancaster in the wartime drama *From Here to Eternity*. Deborah Kerr, who died at 86 from Parkinson's disease, also taught Yul Brynner to dance in *The King and I* and fell in love with Cary Grant in *An Affair to Remember*—and, in 1994, was finally awarded an honorary Academy Award, in recognition of her "perfection, discipline and elegance."

Lady Bird and Lyndon Johnson c. 1964. He proposed on their first date; after he persisted for 10 weeks, she said yes.

1912–2007
July 11

LADY BIRD JOHNSON

She lived though years of tumult and upheaval with disarming southern charm. Claudia "Lady Bird" Taylor Johnson, 94, widow of President Lyndon B. Johnson, died in her home in Austin, Texas, after a brief illness. The lifelong nature enthusiast was laid to rest next to her husband beneath a canopy of oak trees in the family cemetery in Stonewall, Texas. "My special cause," Lady Bird (a childhood nickname) once said, "... is to preserve the wildflowers and native plants that define the regions of our land and [pass on] the quiet joys and satisfactions I have known since my childhood."

ART BUCHWALD

Hours after Art Buchwald passed away, the following message appeared on his Web site: "Hi, I'm Art Buchwald, and I just died." A comedian to the end, Buchwald even died funny.

The beloved humorist, whose Pulitzer Prize-winning column was, at its peak, syndicated in more than 500 newspapers, had been terminally ill with kidney failure for a year—and giving interviews about it. "Dying isn't hard," he observed at one point. "Getting paid by Medicare is." Typically, he offered gentle wisdom as well. "If you can make people laugh," he said, "you're getting all the love you want."

1925–2007
January 17

Buchwald, said his daughter Jennifer, loved people: "He would talk to any stranger."

1922–2007 ●
April 11

Kurt Vonnegut

During the '60s, his novels—*Cat's Cradle, Mother Night, God Bless You, Mr. Rosewater*—were in every backpack; *Slaughterhouse-Five*, his fictionalized account of his WWII experiences as an American POW during the firebombing of Dresden, Germany, was an apocalyptic masterpiece. Sweet-souled, world-weary and funny, Kurt Vonnegut clung to a philosophy succinctly expressed by his fictional alter ego, Eliot Rosewater: "God damn it, you've got to be kind." He died, at 84, after falling in his apartment and suffering brain injuries.

Beverly Sills

1929–2007
July 2

Asked about her glowing reception in Milan in 1969, Beverly Sills joked, "It's probably because Italians like big women, big bosoms and big backsides."

The Brooklyn-born soprano, who died of lung cancer at 78, was the diva next door, comfortable at the Met or on *The Muppet Show*. Still, said her friend Barbara Walters, "her public life was glorious, but her private life was marked by tragedy."

Both of Sills' children were born with disabilities: Daughter Meredith, 47, is deaf; son Peter Jr., 46, was institutionalized at age 6 and considered mentally retarded ("They knew nothing about autism then," she wrote years later). Sills worked with the March of Dimes to improve infant health. "If she gave a recital, she would always end softly, with kind of a lullaby almost, as if her children were listening," a friend recalled. "As she once told her vocal coach, 'I want to sing so high that my daughter can hear it.'"

A remarkable talent who could evoke humor and pathos without saying a word, mime Marcel Marceau often accomplished "in less than two minutes," one critic wrote, "what most novelists cannot do in volumes." Marceau, who died at 84, learned life's hardest lessons early: As a Jew in WWII France, he joined the Resistance, and his father died at Auschwitz. When the war ended, he discovered pantomime at a school in Paris. "I was," he said, "like a fish in water." Said a former student: "He was a theater company all wrapped up in one person."

1923–2007 ●
September 22

Marcel Marceau

Poston (on *The Bob Newhart Show*) "had fun every day of his life," said his wife, Suzanne Pleshette.

1921–2007
April 30

Tom Poston

As the hapless handyman on *The Bob Newhart Show* or the bumbling boozer on *Mork & Mindy*, Tom Poston specialized in playing characters who were, in his words, "a half-step behind life's parade."

Poston himself, who died at 85 after a brief illness, marched right out front. "You could read everything in his face," said longtime friend Tim Conway. "He could just look at you and you would start laughing."

"He had fun every day of his life," said his widow, former *Newhart* castmate Suzanne Pleshette. "My husband was a delicious man, and I miss him."

"One of my vanities," Mailer once said, "may be that I've always wanted my books to be provocations."

● **1923—2007**
November 10

Norman Mailer

Prolific and pugnacious, Norman Mailer won two Pulitzer Prizes, feuded with fellow writers and feminists, ran for mayor of New York City, wed six times and had nine children. "He presented himself as a tough guy; that was a front," said author Gay Talese. "He had a big heart." But some of the scrapes were real: Famously, at a party in 1960, he stabbed his second wife, Adele, with a penknife. "He never apologized," says Adele, 82. Mailer, who died of kidney failure at 84, broke through in 1948 with *The Naked and the Dead,* inspired by his World War II experiences, and helped reshape the concept of journalism with his "nonfiction novel" *The Armies of the Night* and other books. "People were captivated by the larger than life personality," said writer Doris Kearns Goodwin. "But it's his words that will live on."

Hollywood on ice: Wyman and Reagan c. 1945.

● **1933–2007**
May 15

JERRY FALWELL

Credited with creating one of the nation's first megachurches, Rev. Jerry Falwell, who died at 73 of congestive heart failure, parlayed his success among evangelicals into political pay dirt when he founded the Moral Majority in 1979, registering millions of conservative voters and aiding the landmark election of Ronald Reagan the following year. "Until he became politically active, most conservative Christian leaders felt it was no part of their calling to be involved in the public policy process," said Morton Blackwell, a longtime friend.

Unabashedly controversial, Falwell used his radio and TV appearances to decry homosexuality and abortion rights. After the Sept. 11 terrorist attacks, he said feminists, gays, lesbians and the ACLU had "helped this happen." (He later apologized.) He also described the Antichrist as a Jewish man and warned parents that Tinky Winky, a purse-carrying character on *Teletubbies,* was gay. Said Rev. Barry Lynn of Americans United for Separation of Church and State: "Falwell manipulated a powerful pulpit in exchange for access to political power and promotion of a narrow range of moral concerns . . . but there is no denying his impact on American political life."

Falwell helped make evangelicals a potent political force.

● **1917–2007**
September 10

Jane Wyman

When you first heard of Jane Wyman is, to some degree, a generational litmus test. To very longtime fans, Jane Wyman, who died at 90, is the first wife of former President Ronald Reagan and a Hollywood grand dame who won an Oscar for the 1948 film *Johnny Belinda.* After a long idle period, Wyman made a showbiz comeback and reintroduced herself to a new audience, playing calculating Napa Valley winery owner Angela Channing on the TV drama *Falcon Crest.*

1918–2007 ●
October 17

Joey Bishop

He was, as he himself said, "the mouse in the Rat Pack"—the dour straight man who made his pals Frank Sinatra, Dean Martin, Peter Lawford and Sammy Davis Jr. appear even funnier. Making others look good may have even been Joey Bishop's special gift: After careening with the boys through Las Vegas and costarring in the original *Ocean's 11*, Bishop, who died at 89, hosted his own TV variety show and subbed for Johnny Carson on *The Tonight Show* about 200 times.

A boys' club's golden era: Sammy, Dean, Frank and Joey in 1960.

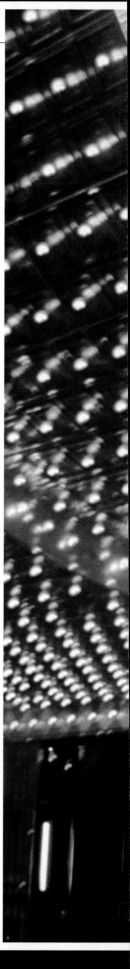

● **1933–2007**
October 30

Robert Goulet

I n 1960 matinée-idol-handsome Robert Goulet, as the dashing Sir Lancelot, became a national heartthrob in the smash Broadway musical *Camelot*, singing "If Ever I Would Leave You" to his Guenevere, played by Julie Andrews. He rode that wave with talent, charm and a self-aware wink—he voiced his own character on *The Simpsons* and recently starred in a commercial for Emerald Nuts—for 50 years. "There wasn't a woman alive whose heart didn't beat faster when he got close," said Leslie Nielsen, who starred with Goulet in the movie *The Naked Gun 2 ½*. "There was a kaleidoscope of talents resting in there." He died at 73 of pulmonary fibrosis.

"You be good"

—Alex

September 6

Alex the Parrot

He was a bird brain, and he had reason to be proud. Alex, an African gray parrot, learned shapes, colors and more than 100 English words with the help of Dr. Irene Pepperberg, a comparative psychologist. Scientists were amazed, and lay people amused, by Alex's command of language and ability to learn. "The work revolutionized the way we think about bird brains," Diana Reiss, a psychologist, told *The New York Times*. "That used to be a pejorative, but now we look at those brains—at least Alex's—with some awe."

One night in September, Dr. Pepperberg put Alex, 31, in his cage for the evening. "You be good; see you tomorrow," Alex said, according to the *Times*. "I love you."

The next morning Alex was found dead of natural causes.

Winning by 6½ lengths, Barbaro seemed a superhorse at the 2006 Kentucky Derby.

Barbaro stunned the horse-racing world, and even casual fans, when he won the Kentucky Derby by 6½ lengths in May 2006. Two weeks later he shattered his right hind leg at the Preakness Stakes. For more than eight months, vets tried everything and anything to save him; then, when complications from the original injury made even standing painful, owners Roy and Gretchen Jackson made an agonizing decision. Barbaro was euthanized. "Certainly," Gretchen said, "grief is the price we all pay for love."

● **2003–2007**
January 29

Barbaro